Forever Better

Continuous Quality Improvement in Higher Education

Peter Knight
E. Nola Aitken
Robert J. Rogerson

NEW FORUMS PRESS INC.

Stillwater, Oklahoma U.S.A.

ISBN: 1-58107-024-1

Forever Better

Contents

About the Book

This book is a no-nonsense approach to teaching improvement that is geared to the needs of hard-pressed faculty in higher education. Although it is primarily intended for established faculty members who want to improve their teaching despite limited time, it will also have important ideas for chairs, heads of department and new faculty members, professional staff and teaching assistants.

Forever Better draws on research evidence and practice in North America, Britain, New Zealand and Australia to present a host of well-tried, well-conceived 'pick and mix' ideas that can help anyone to be better at teaching. It covers major themes such as course planning, assessing student learning, lecturing, working with small groups and handling large classes, and covers the use of established and new technologies and methods to bring about improvements.

The book is based on long and continuing experience of undergraduate teaching in a range of universities. Consequently, it contains a good number of established and new teaching technologies and methods. It recommends that you try and become a better teacher a piece at a time, using well tried ideas at a comfortable rate. It uses research findings but wears them lightly: jargon, obscure disputes and extensive citations are avoided. It has a practical tone. For example, one of the principles on which the authors insist is that it is best to identify one area of teaching as a priority for improvement and in any academic year concentrate on it alone: realism is the watchword.

About the Authors

Dr. Peter T. Knight has worked in the Department of Educational Research at Lancaster University, UK, since 1990. He was previously the Head of the Department of History at St. Martin's College of Higher Education, Lancaster, UK.

Dr. E. Nola Aitken has been an Assistant Professor in the Faculty of Education, The University of Lethbridge since 1992. She previously spent 21 years as an elementary and secondary teacher, two years as a school jurisdiction administrator, and 5 years as a Mathematics Test Development Specialist for the Ministry of Education in Alberta.

Dr. Robert J. Rogerson has been Professor in the Department of Geography, The University of Lethbridge, since 1988. He was formerly Dean of Arts and Science at The University of Lethbridge and before that, Professor of Geography and Earth Sciences at Memorial University of Newfoundland, Head of Geography, Assistant Director of the Labrador Institute, Executive Director of Oceans 2000 Secretariat and subsequently Executive Director of the Canadian Center for GIS in Education in Ottawa. His academic field is Glaciology and Glacial Geomorphology.

1. Forever Better

Who are we writing for?

This is not a book for bad teachers, although they will find it useful. It is primarily a book for

- Mid-career faculty
- New faculty
- Teaching assistants
- Departmental Chairs and administrators

We competent teachers need a book like this for three reasons:

- The conditions in which we work are changing: classes are larger, calls on our time multiply, students are often different from those we taught ten years ago.
- What we are expected to teach is changing. In many English-speaking countries, we are asked to promote general skills and qualities, as well as understanding of and affection for our subjects.
- We can always improve the quality of what we do, and it is in our interests, as we shall show, to do that, in teaching, in service, and in research.

Continuous quality improvement

In effect, we are talking about continuous quality improvement. You will know about quality control (which is about fixing defects), and about quality assurance (which is about designing high quality into a product, such as an undergraduate program). We agree that things like course evaluations are necessary to pick up defects in teaching (quality control), and that good program design is essential (quality assurance). More important still is continuous quality improvement (CQI)—or "forever better," as we have called it.

CQI is a concept that was developed in for-profit organizations. Three key features are:

- Improvements can always be made and should always be looked for. Interestingly, this is close, in its spirit, to the idea of "reflective practice," which has influenced many teacher educators, and staff and instructional development professionals. It is the idea that we should reflect on our practice, looking for improvements, which are sometimes small (playing some Mozart just before a presentation begins), and sometimes large (wondering whether what we teach is giving the students the best we have to offer).

- People should be empowered. That means they should feel free to take the initiative, to take risks, and to use their best judgment.
- People work together. This does not mean that your independence is taken away. It does mean that you talk with colleagues and are aware of the relationship between what they do and what you do. People consult, share, discuss, and support each other.

We see CQI as a powerful concept to apply to our work as teachers in higher education. It means that rather than thinking of ourselves as isolated agents, we think more in terms of individuals within a team, in this case the team of people teaching an undergraduate, master's, or doctoral program. In Japanese, it is called *Kaizen*, and has been described as the key to Japan's competitive success. We take the same view of its importance in higher education.

Research comes first?

Peter, Nola, and Robert are all classroom teachers. We are also expected to research and publish. It is from that standpoint that we look at a possible objection to what we are saying, namely the objection that teaching has to be a matter of coping, not of CQI, simply in order to get research done and to attend the flocks of committees that have come to roost upon higher education. We return to this research-teaching tension in Chapter 8 and in question 1 of Chapter 9.

There is no doubt that faculty's workload has intensified: we do more, teach more students, cope with greater expectations, and usually wear more hats (have more roles) than was the case ten years ago. That is not the work of particularly exploitative administration in any one university, but an international fact of academic life. At the same time, appointment, tenure, renewal, and promotion decisions are often dominated by discussion of a person's research and publications profile. As long as this is the case, surely it makes sense to teach with as little effort as is consistent with reasonable student evaluations?

We offer three reasons for thinking that teaching does not have to be a distraction from research, beginning with the point that teaching is a requirement of almost all academic posts; that governments, which provide the majority of funding to public universities, are expecting to see better quality teaching; and that it is necessary, not optional, to look for ways of bringing the two activities into some harmony.

Secondly, problems are reduced where teaching echoes the themes of current research. It can even complement that research. An undergraduate course on a research area is not only enhanced by the enthusiasm and insight that come from the research, but can also contribute to that research in at least two ways. One is based on the saying that to teach is to learn twice. Having to teach about something you are researching is a very powerful way of clarifying your thinking about it. The other way is by having students do mini-research projects within their course. One of us has them analyzing research data and doing their own small-scale research, or literature reviews on one aspect of his research topic. The students' work complements the main research program.

Thirdly, this book contains a number of suggestions for teaching well *and* efficiently. Mindful teaching can take less of your time than simply doing things the way they have always been done.

Benefits

> ... human terrestrial locomotion is most efficient when *walking* at between 4.5 and 5 kilometers per hour ... Above [8.3 kilometers per hour] *running* has lower energy cost than walking, and while the cost of walking keeps on increasing with speeds above 1.3 meters per second, the cost of *running* does not vary significantly with speeds between 2.3 and 6 meters per second [8.3 km/h and 21.6 km/h]. (Smil, 1999, p. 88, emphases in original)

We want to suggest that teaching better is rather like running not walking. There is no doubt that strolling at just over 3 miles per hour (4.5-5 km/h) is highly efficient, just like the pattern of teaching that instructors around the globe settle in to. However, if you are ambitious and want to go faster—to teach better—it becomes progressively harder to keep with walking—to try to fine-tune the default model of teaching. It is a model that is good for some basic things and progressively less appropriate for developing higher level skills, understanding and qualities.

Going faster on your own two legs is a lot easier if you make a phase change and start running. For sure, many of us are not used to running and it takes time to learn. It usually involves learning to use different sets of muscles, which hurts, and is tiring; breathing differently, which is uncomfortable; and having sore feet. So, after a rather gruesome time learning to run, and it may be shorter or longer, you find that you can cover quite long distances under your own steam at a good speed: probably not at 6 meters/second but probably at 3 meters/second (just under 7 mph or 11 km/h. Likewise with better teaching. If you want to do more than ice the cake, rearrange the deck chairs on the *Titanic*, or develop a better wireless set, then it means making a phase change. We suggest that the CQI approach to teaching leads to a break with the default pattern of teaching in higher education. It leads to running compared to the pedestrian stroll of the lecture-text-test model. Like running, it takes effort and time. Like running it brings personal benefits (there's an exhilaration reported by runners and good teachers alike, as well as evident personal health). And there are benefits to students and other stakeholders in higher education.

The benefits for students are quite simply better learning. We mean two things by that. The first is that you teach the material better, so they understand it better, learn and remember it better, and can make better use of what they learn. There is evidence that this is more satisfying for students and can even be more enjoyable. The second thing we have in mind is that the scope of the teaching becomes wider. Most of us have course aims or goals that include helping students to be better at analyzing, criticizing, drawing information together (synthesizing), and evaluating. Many also want to help students to communicate better in writing and orally, to be more self-reliant, and to help them to work in groups and teams. For us, better learning means taking those aims seriously, so that students continue to master the material, but they do so by working in ways that really do foster such general skills and qualities. The reasons why this is good for students include the fact that employers and graduate schools are keen to recruit people with exactly these qualities and skills. A sample of these broader aims is contained in Table 1.1. Further discussion of them is to be found in Barnett (1994), Harvey and Knight (1996) and Jones (1996).

The benefits for you are instrumental as well as intrinsic. The instrumental rewards are in better student evaluations and improved success in promotion, tenure and renewal applications. The intrinsic benefits that are often reported include greater satisfaction and sense of fulfillment.

The institution benefits from happy students and from faculty who find teaching a source of enjoyment, rather than a cause of depression or distress. And where better teaching is understood as teaching that encourages the development of general qualities and skills, the students do better in the labor market, which is also good for the institution. We add that in some countries, improving the quality of teaching, as we have described it, is mandatory, and institutions that do not take teaching seriously face a tough time from government. We return to the question of why it is worth taking teaching seriously in Chapter 9, question 2.

Showing this in a teaching portfolio

In many universities, faculties have to submit a teaching portfolio in support of an application for renewal, tenure, and promotion. New hires have to show evidence of teaching quality in order to get appointed. Table 1.2 lists the main

Table 1.1
General Skills and Qualities That Might Be Fostered
by a Higher Education Program

Intellectual Skills	Practical Skills	Personal Skills and Qualities	Social or Interpersonal Skills and Qualities
Logical thinking	Research skills and methods	Independence/self-reliance	Teamwork
Critical reasoning	Practical skills in laboratory or workshop situations	Self-motivation	Leadership
Understanding and applying concepts	Practical skills in field, community, or employment situations	Planning and organizational skills	Networking
Flexibility and adaptability	Information processing skills	Self -regulation, working within norms and codes	Communication
Problem-solving	Content/textual analysis skills	Adherence to moral/ethical values	Negotiation
Analysis and interpretation	Performance skills	Enterprise and resourcefulness	Client focus
Synthesis	Design skills	Self-preservation	Empathy
Originality	Production skills	Emotional resilience	Ethical practice
Other	Interview skills	Reflective practitioner	Social awareness
	Professional skills	Other	Environmental awareness
	Other		Other

sections of a typical teaching portfolio and makes links between this book and a teaching portfolio. Boxes 8.5-8.7 provide more ideas.

It cannot be overemphasized that a teaching portfolio is not a collection of sources, such as student evaluations, peer comments, and letters of appreciation. It is a reflected collection of **evidence** that supports claims that you make. These claims must be clear and up-front. They should also pervade the portfolio.

Table 1.2
Teaching Portfolios

Teaching Portfolio Section	Link With This Book
Overview	• Show that you take a CQI approach to learning. • Outline what is in the portfolio and say how it is evidence of quality teaching. This reflective practice is the most important part of the portfolio, since here you make out your case.
Teaching Aims or Goals	• It goes without saying that you aim to make your teaching interesting, comprehensible, enjoyable, and something that leads to deep understanding. • It's also important to draw attention to general qualities and skills that you foster. Refer to table 1.1.
Evidence of Skill in Teaching	• A good introduction might include a general appraisal of your teaching quality by your Chair, and reports of peer evaluations and assessments. • You should highlight outstanding skills that you have. • Then, you could use the headings of chapters 3-7 to organize your evidence. • Begin each section with a summary of the evidence and say what you think it shows. • Evidence is anything that can be used as evidence: student evaluations, letters, notes and comments. (See also Box 8.6). • Highlight both innovative practice and changes you have made in your teaching.
Evidence of Course and Program Planning	• Draw on Chapters 2 and 3 for this. • If you include a course syllabus (as an appendix), draw attention to distinctive features of the course and things that represent good practice and thinking in course design. • If students find the course syllabus (which may be on the web) helpful, include some of their comments.
Professional Development Activities (Teaching)	• Reading this book is a professional development activity ... • ... as is a commitment to CQI. • Add details of courses and conferences on teaching that you have attended or participated in: make a big play of any teaching presentations you have done for other departments or universities. • Mention again in-house curriculum development and activities to improve teaching: doing is itself an important form of professional development.
Publications on Teaching and Learning	• List them. There is a ready audience for articles describing good practice and innovation in teaching within an academic subject. In many universities they are recognized as a legitimate research product.
Plans	• This book may give you ideas for directions for future development. Tables 1.3 and 1.4 may be especially relevant.

More detailed, good advice is offered by Seldin, 1995, and O'Neil and Wright, 1995.

Articles of faith and aspirations

Two beliefs and two aspirations run through this book. One article of faith is that we wish to encourage "deep" approaches to learning. This notion is familiar outside North America but not as well known within it. Deep approaches involve students seeking meaning, aiming to understand and, in the process, working on material to reorganize it in ways that make sense to them. Deep approaches are encouraged by tasks that are not routine and by learning environments that encourage risk-taking, allow a degree of student autonomy and where it is acceptable to make mistakes (Entwistle, Marton & Hounsell, 1997). "Surface" approaches are diametrically opposite. The students' aim is to memorize and regurgitate information. Understanding is not wanted and is not encouraged by the tasks. Ironically, this approach to learning is self-defeating, since knowledge is best retained and retrieved from memory when it has been understood and thought about. These ideas are revisited in Chapter 2 and summarized in Table 2.2.

The second is that we wish to see students consciously learning a range of general skills and developing their personal qualities while they are going about the normal, natural business of learning for understanding of their subject matter. Good teaching is, then, teaching that has broad goals.

To these two articles of faith we add two aspirations. The first is that teachers will increasingly talk with each other about teaching and student learning. Our understanding of organizations is that where there is cooperation and collaboration, the organization is more efficient and more effective. We hope to see this influencing departments and faculties in higher education. Useful summaries of current management thinking are in the books by Allee, 1997; Morgan, 1997; and Wenger, 1998.

The second follows on from the theme of collaboration. It is based on systems thinking. The hope is that faculty will increasingly think, plan, and teach with complete programs in mind. Students follow programs that comprise courses. Where programs are well planned, then the courses come together and support and reinforce each other. In this way, student learning is enhanced. There is a great potential for improving student learning when we think as much about the complete student experience (that is to say, of programs), rather than just in terms of "my course." The suggestions we make in this book have to be things that are within your direct control but we repeatedly point out that some things would work a lot better if they were part of a program-wide plan.

Where are you now?

Table 1.3 is a questionnaire designed to help you clarify the best place to start in tuning your teaching.

Some may choose to read this book from cover to cover. Many, we feel, would like to identify an area in which to begin the business of tuning teaching quality. This table is designed to help in that process. Teaching Assistants and new faculty should also read Chapter 8 before going any further.

Our CQI suggestions are based on our knowledge of the international research literature, and on our combined experience of over 80 years of teaching, at all levels. We have not cluttered our suggestions with a host of references, concentrating on the most important sources of ideas.

We have also restricted the advice we give. Improving teaching can be a very far-reaching project that involves change to ourselves, as people, as well as changes in the organization and operation of departments, faculties, and universities. In this book, we have concentrated on practical things that you can do to make a difference. The aim is to offer advice that contains things that are immediately useful. We do this knowing that the path of CQI means that more complex, entangled, value-soaked, and larger-scale matters should eventually get attention. But not in this book. In Chapter 9, though, we offer responses to three questions that are often pressing concerns for teachers (questions 3, 4 & 5), while in the following chapters present a more thoroughgoing treatment of ways of fine-tuning your teaching practices.

With that, we suggest you read Table 1.3 and then complete the scoring grid (Table 1.4).

Table 1.3. Finding a Starting Place

The course plan, syllabus and handbook

1. Have student evaluations made you think this needs attention?
2. Have the comments of colleagues made you think this needs attention?
3. Have you improved this within the past two years?
4. Does the course syllabus have broad aims (including the development of general skills and qualities)?
5. Are the teaching methods appropriate as ways of supporting the aims?
6. Are the assessment methods appropriate as ways of supporting the aims?
7. Are assessment criteria set out in detail in the syllabus?
8. Are the readings annotated so that students know why they are asked to read a key piece, and have an idea of how important it is in relation to other readings on the topic?

The student learning environment (expectations about student learning)

1. Have student evaluations made you think this needs attention?
2. Have the comments of colleagues made you think this needs attention?
3. Have you improved this within the past two years?
4. Do students have choice, either of topic, or of assessment tasks, or of the ways in which they are assessed?
5. Are students able to work, to some degree, at their own pace?
6. Are students encouraged to collaborate?
7. Do students understand the idea of deep approaches to learning?
8. Are useful resources readily available to students in sufficient quantities?

Assessing student learning (also known as grading, marking, testing and evaluation)

1. Have student evaluations made you think this needs attention?
2. Have the comments of colleagues made you think this needs attention?
3. Have you improved your assessment practices within the past two years?
4. Do you have an assessment plan or blueprint for your course?
5. Do you use a variety of assessment methods, techniques or tools?
6. Is all grading done by you or other faculty?
7. Do students get feedback and guidance on their work that is designed to help them to do better next time?
8. Are students' marks based on individual unaided pieces of work?

Presentations (formerly known as lectures)

1. Have student evaluations made you think this needs attention?
2. Have the comments of colleagues made you think this needs attention?
3. Have you improved this within the past two years?

Table 1.3. Finding a Starting Place (cont.)

4. Do you take time to relax before presentations?
5. Do you essentially read a lecture in your presentation?
6. Is your main goal in presentations to convey information?
7. Do you have breaks or changes of activity in your presentations?
8. Do you use Classroom Assessment Techniques in your presentations?

Working with groups

1. Have student evaluations made you think this needs attention?
2. Have the comments of colleagues made you think this needs attention?
3. Have you improved this within the past two years?
4. Do you encourage students to collaborate on out-of-class tasks?
5. Do you set group tasks that will contribute to the course grade?
6. Are there group activities within your seminars, tutorials, or lectures?
7. Are students taught how to work in groups?
8. Have you read any of the literature on when group work is useful, and how to organize groups to best effect?

Working with large classes

1. Have student evaluations made you think this needs attention?
2. Have the comments of colleagues made you think this needs attention?
3. Have you improved this within the past two years?
4. Has your large class course been completely replanned with the special needs of large classes in mind?
5. Have you explored ways of reducing the time you spend on grading the work of students in large classes?
6. Are your large classes organized so that there are presentations to the whole class and smaller seminar/tutorial meetings to complement them?
7. Do the people who lead the seminars/tutorials understand that a major goal of these sessions is to make students feel that here is someone who is ***their*** tutor, a dependable point of contact?
8. Have you taken a class or got other help to improve your presentation techniques (voice projection, body language, design and use of overhead projector transparencies, pacing a presentation, etc.)?

Table 1.4
Scoring Grid

First check the "yes" or "no" in the appropriate columns. Then, for each statement, consider how important an aspect of teaching you think it to be. In the corresponding "Value" columns put **2** if it is something you think is important and **1** if it is not so important. Total the numbers in the "Value" colums for each section, noting the + and – signs. The section with the highest score is, we suggest, the one to start on.

Question	Check if Yes	Value	Check if No	Value
Course Syllabus		+		-
1. Student evaluations		+		-
2. Peer comments		-		+
3. Improved over past 2 years?		-		+
4. Broad aims?		-		+
5. Teaching methods fit aims?		-		+
6. Assessment methods fit aims?		-		+ ·
7. Detailed assessment criteria?		-		+
8. Readings annotated?		-		+
Total score for course syllabus	Either plus _____ or minus _____			
Student Learning Environment				
1. Student evaluations		+		-
2. Peer comments		+		-
3. Improved over past 2 years?		-		+
4. Student choice		-		+
5. Students work at own pace?		-		+
6. Collaboration encouraged?		-		+
7. Deep learning?		-		+
8. Resources?		-		+
Total score for SLE	Either plus _____ or minus _____			

Table 1.4
Scoring Grid (cont.)

Question	Check if Yes	Value	Check if No	Value
Assessing Student Learning				
1. Student evaluations		+		-
2. Peer comments		+		-
3. Improved over past 2 years?		-		+
4. Have assessment plan?		-		+
5. Use a variety of assessment methods?		-		+
6. Faculty do the grading		+		-
7. Formative feedback for students		-		+
8. Only individual work counts		+		-
Total score for assessing	Either plus _____ or minus _____			
Presentations				
1. Student evaluations		+		-
2. Peer comments		+		-
3. Improved over past 2 years?		-		+
4. Relax before?		-		+
5. Read out a lecture		+		-
6. Convey information		+		-
7. Breaks and change of activities		-		+
8. Use CATs		-		+
Total score for presentations	Either plus _____ or minus _____			

Table 1.4
Scoring Grid (cont.)

Question	Check if Yes	Value	Check if No	Value
Working with groups				
1. Student evaluations		+		-
2. Peer comments		+		-
3. Improved over past 2 years?		-		+
4. Out of class collaboration?		-		+
5. Graded group tasks?		-		+
6. Group activities in seminars, etc?		-		+
7. Students taught to work in groups?		-		+
8. Read relevant literature?		-		+
Total score for groupwork	Either plus _____ or minus _____			
Large classes				
1. Student evaluations		+		-
2. Peer comments		+		-
3. Improved over past 2 years?		-		+
4. Course re-planned?		-		+
5. Less time spent on grading?		-		+
6. Complementary seminars?		-		+
7. Seminar tutor goals		-		+
8. Improved presentation technique?		-		+
Total score for classes	Either plus _____ or minus _____			

PRIORITY AREA = SECTION WITH HIGHEST SCORE.

Worked example:

Question	Check if Yes	Value	Check if No	Value
Large classes				
1. Student evaluations	✓	+2		-
2. Peer comments		+	✓	-1
3. Improved over past 2 years?		-	✓	+1
4. Course re-planned?	✓	-2		+
5. Less time spent on grading?		-	✓	+1
6. Complementary seminars?	✓	-1		+
7. Seminar tutor goals		-	✓	+1
8. Improved presentation technique?		-	✓	+1
Total score for classes	Either plus __2__ or minus _____			

This tutor thought that the two most important questions were about student evaluations and course revision. Each of those was weighted at 2, and the rest were rated at 1. Summing the answers with a plus figure gave a value of +6, the minus figure being -4. The overall score for this section is +2.

If the scores for the other four sections were 0, -1, -2 and 0, then this would still be the one to start thinking about, since it has the highest score (= +1). However, if the other section scores were +3, +2, -1 and 0, then the section with the score of +3 would be the one to start with.

2. The Student Learning Environment

Preview

This is a chapter mainly about the ways in which expectations and assumptions can encourage and discourage different types of learning and learner. These expectations and assumptions—in other words, these learning environments—can:

- Encourage students to practice some approaches to learning, such as surface or "deep" approaches, rather than others.
- Stimulate students to prefer some learning behaviors rather than others.
- Favor people who are intelligent on traditional measures or resonate with people who have different intellectual strengths.
- Affect students' drive to learn and their explanations of any learning difficulties they encounter.

Seven ideas for better teaching that can be derived from this review of learning environments are these:

1. Plan so that students are always asked to look for meaning. That often means treating less material in greater depth.
2. It is a truism to say that interesting material should always be preferred. Some times truisms need to be remembered.
3. Explain to students why what they are doing is important; why you teach as you do; about what the thinking is behind your grading practices; why you want web seminars; and so on.
4. Use a variety of teaching and assessment methods to reflect the many forms of diversity in your class.
5. Give students choice, wherever it is possible, so that they can play to strengths.
6. Set things up for student success.
7. Where students fall short, help them to attribute it to things that can be fixed, with time and effort.

Learning is our business

If asked about our work as professors, most of us would say that it is dominated by research and teaching, which shows how wrong we can be. For sure, most faculty are expected to do research and to publish. We are also expected to teach. But universities and colleges are not really in the business of instruction. They are in the business of learning: of learning through research and of helping students to learn. What we usually call "teaching" or "instruction" is a highly visible part of universities' attempts to help students to learn. However, many things apart from "teaching" contribute to—or impede—learning. Good instruction involves being sensitive to the conditions that make for good learning, to the student learning environment.

Fear and learning

The amygdala is a part of the brain that challenges every situation a person faces to see if it's safe. It's the part of the brain that triggers the flight or fight hormones when it detects a dangerous situation and it is responsible for heightening the reactivity of key brain areas, particularly the senses. When the flight or fight emotion has been triggered, creative and rational thought take a back seat because when the body is under stress,

- Blood flows to the large muscles and the posture locks;
- Hearing becomes attuned to danger signals and other messages get missed (which is why stressed people find it hard to follow conversations);
- Visual focus becomes less controlled;
- Cortisol levels increase, which reduces learning and memory capacity (and frequently-stressed people will not want to know that elevated cortisol levels are associated with accelerated aging);
- Upper brain beta waves are more pronounced, again at the expense of learning.

This is why some good students don't do well on tests because they have a fear of them. When the amygdala is taking care of the student's survival, then its chemical messengers to the body are actually getting in the way of the student getting an A grade. But if the student really had to bolt for the door, he would probably stand a better chance than most to reach the door first if the amygdala were in control. Unfortunately, we do not get A grades for that.

Now, we are not saying that good learning environments are stress-free. We are saying that most people have had teachers who have unintentionally or not, made them afraid in the classroom; afraid of saying the wrong thing and being publicly ridiculed, or being admonished for an inappropriate response, for example. The atmosphere is tense and uncomfortable. Most students in that kind of atmosphere cannot do their best, nor are they motivated; they just want the class over and done with and make good their escape to friendlier turf. Without a comfortable atmosphere in the classroom, the lesson is likely to fall flat, no matter how well prepared it is. So, we are saying that one way of fine-tuning your teaching practices is to try to design some of the most commonly stressful factors out of the environment. Of course, we still need to have challenges in place (we often call them assignments and tests) because good learning environments are low stress but not low demand environments. Whatever the challenges, some will feel them more sharply than others; for instance some people find things such as group work or public speaking to be inherently stressful whereas others lack the sensitivity to realize that they might perform rather better if they did get rather more stressed by them. We cannot guarantee that any approach to classroom teaching will make all of students feel comfortable and at ease, interested in learning but not aroused enough to interfere with learning. We can say that key features of a low stress learning climate are the following:

- Openness about what will be expected and when; about the standards to be applied.
- Evidence or other reassurance that what is asked is quite reasonable and achievable—success is available to those who put sufficient effort into the learning activities.
- Clear details about how to go about the assignments. These do not need to amount to spoon-feeding, but they should constitute fair descriptions of what you need to do in order to succeed with assignments and tests.
- Teachers do not take a stance that suggests that they are there to discover ignorance and stupidity and to fail students. Their stance is that they are there to help students to come to grips with worthwhile material; that success is to be expected; and that help is always available from them, from teaching assistants (TAs) or through peer support. This is seen in the way that teachers speak with students—in little things such as thanking students for questions, or asking for and using their names.
- Teachers smile, make eye contact (but do not ogle), have an easy posture and say that they too have found—and perhaps still do find—some things difficult or puzzling, or counter-intuitive. They look human, sound human, and say human things.

It is quite possible to run a course according to these principles and still have a learning environment that is not conducive to good learning. Good learning certainly is encouraged by the course climate but it depends upon other environmental factors as well.

Two learning environments

Boxes 2.1 and 2.2 describe two "learning environments." As you read them, it will become apparent that we are not using "environment" only in the sense of the physical environment, important though that is. The mental, or cultural, environment is at least as important. In fact, studies of effective schools have tended to show that children's achievement is not related to resources, buildings, and facilities as much as it is to the cultural environment, or ethos.

This is a powerful insight, since there is often little that can be done about the physical environment. The cultural environment is more malleable. For example, studies of effective schools have suggested that those that succeed are ones where the teachers refuse to accept that students' socioeconomic status *determines* their educational progress. These are schools where teachers believe that learning cultures can be formed, regardless of the characteristics of the students, the area, or of the physical environment. Of course, it is easier to create good learning environments in schools with children who are well disposed to learn, but a powerful message of the school improvement literature is that it can be done anywhere.

Money might be in short supply, buildings might leak, faculty time is usually short and libraries are underfunded. Yet, good learning environments can still be created.

2.1. Learning Environment 1: Downtown Metropolitan University

Downtown Metropolitan University was formed in 1993 when two colleges merged to form a state university. It has buildings scattered around the city, some of them converted school buildings, others converted office accommodation. The natural sciences are housed in a bloc that was custom-built in 1972. Space is short, the furnishings and fittings are worn, and classes are often overcrowded and in dreary, shabby rooms. Broken chairs lie beside torn drapes at the back of some rooms, which have the look of places where furnishings go to die. However, the premises are kept clean and security is good, although the on-site food outlets are few and uninspiring.

The university has little residential accommodation and most students live at home and commute. Since many also have to work, the university is at its busiest in the evenings. The Students Union, in association with the Education Department, runs a daycare that is open during university sessions. There is a waiting list for places and some faculty members would like there to be a daycare for their children as well.

The computer equipment is usually rather dated (486s are the norm) and is centralized in heavily-used public access rooms. All students have Internet accounts and some classes are electronic, so that students interact with the teachers and each other through the Internet, when it is convenient for them. Some log in from home.

Academic staff teach more than at the other three universities in the area and have bigger classes. However, there is a strong Instructional Development Office that advises on efficient teaching and faculty tend to integrate their teaching and research, with the result that most faculty are "research active." There is an emphasis on making it easy for students to contact

---

teachers, which is possible only because faculty are available on E-mail and because course syllabuses are written so as to anticipate the most common problems that students face.

Programs have been designed to foster a range of skills and qualities, as well as developing mastery of subject matter, and the calendar shows which courses concentrate on which skills and qualities. Students are encouraged to choose courses out of interest, need, and with an idea of compiling a balanced profile of skill development. This is supported by the publication of clear and detailed evaluation criteria for each course.

●●●●●●●●●

Benny, a junior year student, likes the choice that she has, and has been accustomed from the freshman year, to the idea that she is responsible for the program she puts together. She finds the program and course information useful, if rather intimidating, and has come to like the way that there is choice within courses, as well as between courses. While there is little choice about following the lecture-and-seminar schedule, she can choose the topics on which she is to be assessed, suggest the criteria that would be the fairest way of evaluating her performance, and attach a self-assessment schedule to each term paper. There is also the option of saying what weight should be given to each evaluation item, which allows her to get more credit for the work that she thinks is particularly good or particularly important.

●●●●●●●●●

Gloria is a mature student who has appreciated the positive attitude of faculty members. Teaching does not seem to be a chore for them, although some are plainly tired by eight o'clock in the evening. More important for her is the belief that students can succeed, the way that the criteria of success are clearly laid out, and the variety of teaching and learning methods that are used. Lectures are not bad, but she learns best when information is presented visually, when she can take it at her own pace, when she can talk with others about what she is doing and about difficulties, and where she is not drowned by details. Her experiences at Downtown Met have allowed her to learn without having to change the learning approaches with which she is comfortable. It helps that people are friendly, including faculty, who don't seem to need to show how important they are. There are some real pains, though.

●●●●●●●●●

Greg, a freshman, has benefited from the way in which work is graded. For sure, there are numbers on his work, but the suggestions for improvement have been more helpful, since they've helped him to see ways of doing better on a different topic the next time. The policy of encouraging students to work together in study groups helped him to cope with the volume of work and not get bogged down in detail or depressed by not coping. That wouldn't have worked as well, had it not been for the group work activities in the classes, which have helped him to learn to work as a team member, as well as to get new insights into the material they are trying to understand. Yet, sometimes all this choice and the uncertainty about what the answer is that the prof. really wants worries him, and he thinks of the simpler life in high school, where you wrote down what the teacher said and then gave it back to her.

●●●●●●●●●

All three students have a sense that they are achieving. None of them have outstanding grades, but all have a sense that they are doing better than they were. The variety of learning activities and the sense of having a choice combine with faculty's emphasis on understanding and using information to give them a sense of being more in control of their work. Which can be scary, sometimes.

2.2 Learning environment 2: University of Pinawa.

Extracts from the university calendar:

"The University of Pinawa is set in parkland in modern, well-designed accommodation. The library has the largest collection of books and journals of any university library in the state. All rooms are wired to the Internet and the university is continually upgrading and expanding its computer facilities to prepare students for the millennium. Professional departments are equipped to modern standards, and are often supported by donations from business ... "

"... All freshman and senior year students can have a modern residential room in the award winning 'Ponderosa Building,' and residences are often available for other students. The sports and recreation facilities are extensive and modern. For those who prefer to roam farther afield, the National Park is an hour's drive away and offers more leisure opportunities than you might begin to imagine..."

"... Faculty members are leading researchers in their field ..."

● ● ● ● ● ● ● ● ●

Marg is a senior year student. Her grades are good and she is satisfied that she knows how to keep them high. The trick is to learn what's in the text and to be able to run it back to the professor, adding anything new that's covered in the lectures. It's quite a task to keep up because there are tests and term papers pretty often, but her routine has worked for her. The university has a good reputation because of the research done there and because it only takes freshman who already have good grades. Getting into grad school, which she is considering, should be no problem. Jobs might be a different matter. Some of the ads she's seen ask for evidence of skills that she is sure she has but which she's hardly had to show while at university.

● ● ● ● ● ● ● ● ●

The priority that Pinawa gives to research has governed faculty appointments, so most are committed academics who have had little, if any training in teaching and who reproduce the methods they experienced. They are also people who learned easily and worked hard and see it as a sign that standards are in decline when they see students who are not like them. On the whole, they are well disposed to students and get on well with them but this is not where time is to be invested. The Tenure, Review, and Promotions Committee is known to operate on the basis of people's publications records, so it is efficient and wise to teach in the way that comes naturally. Whenever possible, Teaching Assistants and demonstrators are used, although few can spare time to take the university's teaching training program, since they are under pressure to make their name quickly with their PhDs.

By and large, they see their teaching role as conveying information to help students understand their conception of the topics. So, essentially their didactic pedagogies give students no choice within courses, for the professors know best what matters in their area. Furthermore, evaluations are designed to ensure that students all know the same material, formulae, and practices equally well, and tend to take the form of selected-response tests, also known as true/false and multiple-choice tests. Grades are distributed according to a notion of what proportion of the students ought to get As, Bs, Cs.... This makes for a very competitive atmosphere—needless to say, students are rarely set any collaborative tasks that will be graded and plagiarism is watched for vigilantly. An advantage of this system is that marking can be fast, so the students rapidly get feedback—their grade.

Key themes in the two learning environments

The physical environments differ, and Downtown Metropolitan faculty could reasonably say that they could do a much better job if they had facilities like Pinawa's. However, good facilities can be used to support and consolidate lackluster approaches to student learning.

The two universities also differ in their cultural climates. These differences are summarized in Table 2.1 (p. 22).

Some of the remarks in Table 2.1 will make more sense as this chapter unfolds. However, at this point it can still be said that:

1. The two universities have different learning environments.
2. In both institutions students have to master the subject matter and we could anticipate that the two sets of students will have similar masteries of the subject matter. However, some other outcomes get attention in the one place and not in the other, so there should be differences in the students' learning, *even in the same subject.*
3. The outcomes encouraged by the Downtown Metropolitan approach lie close to those favored by employers (see Table 1.1) and by many professions and graduate schools.
4. We regard the Downtown Metropolitan approach as better.

To develop these points, we need first, to consider differences in learning approaches; secondly, the notion of intelligence; thirdly, the idea of learning behaviors; fourthly, the idea of motivational styles. We will then draw all of this together with suggestions for creating learning environments that favor the sort of outcomes that Downtown Metropolitan promotes.

Differences in learning approaches

Extensive work in England, Sweden, and Australia has suggested that students use one of four learning approaches (Entwistle, Marton & Hounsell, 1997). We do not describe these four as "learning styles," since a style can be seen as something fixed, so that a student will tend to approach all problems in all situations in the same way. However, there is evidence that students choose from these four approaches according to the learning environment they are working in. So, rather than talk of "styles," which suggests inflexibility, we refer to "approaches." Of course, there are preferred learning approaches, so students might fail to pick up cues that a different approach is needed and simply stick with the tried and tested one. Analogously, faculty might do the same with teaching approaches.

Table 2. 1.
Differences Between the Cultural Climates of Downtown Metropolitan and Pinawa Universities

Area of difference	Downtown Metropolitan	Pinawa
Institutional support for teaching	Committed to teaching, although more could be done	Not much commitment to improving teaching (but notice the TA training program)
Faculty orientation to teaching	Committed to it	Benign inertia
View of teaching	Students construct their own understandings.	Students learn faculty's understandings
Faculty disposition to students	Friendly and accessible	Well disposed but remote
Teaching goals	Content mastery plus development of general skills and qualities	Content mastery
Teaching methods	Varied	Normally didactic
Learning methods	Varied learning methods embedded in courses	Limited range
Range of learning behaviors supported	Wide	Narrow
Range of intelligences supported	Student choice means that there is some scope to select courses and tasks matching the strongest intelligence.	Less room for students to match their strongest intelligence to what they are required to do.
Evaluation	A mix of methods used to foster the desired mix of learning outcomes	Monotonous
Student attitude to evaluation	A chore, but it can be interesting and involve collaboration with others.	Hurdles to be jumped faster than anyone else
Clarity of evaluation criteria (hence of course and program goals)	High	The only criterion is how much students know. This is very clear.
Feedback to students	Points to ways of improving work for the next time	Grade only
Learning approaches favored by this climate	Deep	Surface
This climate is best suited to people with the following motivation	Intrinsic (extrinsic for those who just want to make the grade)	Extrinsic (intrinsic for those who like to know a lot).

Many colleagues are aware that there is a range of teaching approaches but still use lecturing as their default option of preference. The four learning approaches are described in Table 2.2.

Table 2.2.
Four Approaches to Learning

Learning approach	Comment
"Apathetic"	This is really a coping approach, which involves doing as little as possible (intentionally or otherwise) to stay up with the course.
"Surface"	The emphasis is on collecting and remembering information, as it is presented. Ironically, memory is more effective when we re-work information for ourselves, rather than simply try to learn it by rote.
"Deep"	The intention is to understand, make meanings and connections. Information is not rote learned but worked over in the process of constructing a personal understanding.
"Strategic"	This involves being very sensitive to the cues given by faculty about what they expect and then using whichever approach will produce it.

A strategic approach is the most versatile, although being able to use it does depend on having mastered both surface and deep approaches. Of those two approaches, it is the deep approach that is the most prized by faculty and employers. When faculty speak of their goals, they will usually talk of critical, analytical, and evaluative things, which are ways of describing what we have called "working over" information. Employers value these things too.

However, the deep approach is hard to encourage (and hard for many people to develop) because:

- High school teaching has often encouraged surface learning.
- There is a tendency in our culture to believe that information is, of itself, valuable (see quiz shows, for example).
- Deep approaches require that people have learned to analyze, criticize and evaluate. However, these skills are seldom directly taught and are not easy to learn independently.
- Faculty often fail to make it clear when they are looking for deep approaches.
- Evaluation or assessment methods that tacitly encourage surface approaches are common. Suitable evaluation methods *can* encourage learners to adopt "deep" approaches. However, these methods are often demanding in faculty time and produce scores that are not as reliable as those from multiple choice tests. Furthermore, students can complain, because these methods are unfamiliar and threatening to them (see Chapter 4).

In the last section of this chapter we shall make some suggestions for creating a learning environment that is conducive to deep approaches to learning.

Intelligences

Deep approaches to learning involve a quest for understanding. In part, that is a matter of motivation. However, understanding is more likely when learners can use the intelligence they have, and where they can work in a style with which they are familiar. Learners differ in the nature of the intelligence they have and in their habitual ways of learning. So, a good learning environment is one that offers something to all learners, or that does the best it can within the limits set by the goals of the discipline, program and course.

For example, it is often assumed that there is one type of intelligence, general intelligence, which psychologists often call G. The person with a high level of G is expected to perform intelligently across all tasks. There are many problems with this view, three of which are of special interest here.

- Human performance turns out to be very task-specific. High G is not as good a predictor of performance on a task as is sound understanding of the academic domain in which the task is located and of tasks of a similar nature.
- Intelligence tests are not very good as predictors of human success: it has been said that 'emotional intelligence' (Cooper & Sawaf, 1996; Sternberg, 1997) is a far better predictor.
- The measures of G tend to be artificial: it has been said that intelligence is only what intelligence tests measure.

There are three implications for our work as university teachers. One is that if we wish to encourage students to learn things that will have what we call "life value," then it is not enough to concentrate on those aspects that are measured by tests of G. The second is that we might therefore think of "intelligences," not simply of "intelligence." Thirdly, courses that use a variety of teaching, learning and evaluation methods might allow people who have high "intelligence," but not high G, to succeed.

We develop these points by summarizing the work of Howard Gardner (1983). He argued that it is better to think of multiple intelligences than of G. He initially suggested that people have seven forms of intelligence (later extended to eight), although he admits that the figure is somewhat arbitrary—a case could be made for nine or thirteen. His main point stands, namely that people have multiple intelligences, although all eight, nine, or however many, are not all equally developed, with one or two tending to predominate. Table 2.3 summarizes them and they are discussed further in question 6 in Chapter 9.

Table 2.3.
Gardner's Eight Intelligences (1996)

Intelligence	Suitable learning activities
Linguistic (found in journalists, novelists, copywriters, orators)	Journal writing; story-telling, debate and discussions; reading stories.
Logical-mathematical (engineers, lawyers, accountants, scientists and mathematicians)	Solving problems that have a correct answer; analysis, data interpretation; computation and mathematics; logically-structured activities.
Visual/spatial (artists, designers, chess players, pure mathematicians and theoretical physicists)	Making mental maps; using and making videos, posters, representations; using and making metaphors.
Musical (musicians)	Play mood music before (perhaps during) classes; convey understandings in song or music.
Kinesthetic (athletes, dancers, performers, sports people, mechanics)	Use "hands-on" activities; use breaks to change position; act out the learning; use relaxation exercises.
Interpersonal (sales people, managers, politicians, people in caring professions)	Co-operative learning; peer tutoring and peer assessment; presentations; learning through socializing; empathizing.
Intrapersonal (self-understanding)	Reflection on the ways in which learning and achievement are accomplished; directing attention to the emotions-intellect interplay; interpersonal activities.
Naturalistic (botanists, chefs, farmers, occupations)	Ordering, classifying, pattern-seeking; reflection on how nature is involved in the order of things in the world.

Programs that are influenced by the multiple intelligences view are likely to use a broader range of learning, teaching and evaluation methods, so as to cater to people with different intelligences and to allow them to show their achievements in the ways with which they are most comfortable. Based on this analysis, the more that we use a variety of ways to communicate ideas, information, and procedures, the more students we will reach. In this way, more students are nudged towards "deep" approaches to learning, since the teaching is sensitive to their strengths, making "deep" processing of information an easier task for them.

Learning behaviors

As with learning approaches, learning behaviors are not fixed. The tasks we set and the expectations that we convey can induce learners to adopt different styles, although they will usually have preferred behaviors that reflect their personality and experience of schooling. Table 2.4, which draws on Grasha's *Learning with Style* (1996), summarizes common learning behaviors.

Table 2.4.
A Typology of Learning Behaviors

Learning Behavior	Comments
Competitive	Desire to out-perform others. Usually look for acknowledgment.
Collaborative	Like to work with others and to learn from (and with) them.
Avoidant	It's not clear what they're doing at university!
Participant	Enjoy classes and active in them. Keen!
Dependent	Look for a great deal of structure and guidance. Not happy with ambiguity or uncertainty.
Independent	They decide what they want to learn and often learn it in ways that suit them, not necessarily those that faculty want or expect.

The behaviors do overlap, so a competitive learner might also be a participant (although less so if participation will give rivals any advantage), and dependent students might be avoidant in classes that emphasize learning and thinking for oneself.

We return to avoidant students in the next section. The other five behaviors all have their advantages and are all more or less appropriate, depending on the task, the setting, and the purpose. This suggests that programs might be planned to contain learning activities that are best approached now by one behavior, now by another. The message is again one to do with variety.

However, a dependent student will not become an independent student simply because there are activities that require independence. Nor will collaborative activities alone make a collaborative student out of a competitor. Students who are expected to do work that requires a different learning behavior from their habitual one can—and do—rebel by criticizing the activities for being worthless, or by complaining that the teachers are not doing their jobs. Doyle's analysis of tasks set in schools (1983) suggests that learners are anxious to do the work and to get grades that match their efforts. Unfamiliar tasks are ambiguous (the rules for succeeding are not known) and risky (the danger of failing is higher), so the learners will tend to ask the teacher what to do, to be less happy with unfamiliar tasks, and are more likely to become disruptive. For this reason it is quite tempting for the teacher to stay with safer, less ambiguous and less demanding learning activities; after all, not many faculty get bad student evaluations because they set work that is unambitious and undemanding. The effects of this reaction to uncertainty are well known in research into schools, which has shown that teachers often fail to implement challenging new curricula because the students create so many problems, almost as a protest at having to do work in a style that is unfamiliar to them.

It is understandable to respond to this by deciding to stick with work for students, which is safe. However, the cost is in complicity with the view that the job of universities is simply to develop content knowledge, rather than to develop students in as many ways as possible.

If better teaching is about helping students to use, deliberately, a range of behaviors, then resistance must be anticipated. It can be lessened in the following ways:

- By explaining to students the goals of the course and program and making their value clear. This is not a one-time activity, but something that needs to be repeated throughout a course and a program.
- By making sure that students learn what it is to use different learning behaviors. The authors have conducted research into independent learning and have concluded that for most people, becoming more independent (which is something highly valued by graduate schools and employers) involves first working within a structure that makes it safe to develop the qualities needed in order to be able to work independently. Where students are simply expected to pick up unfamiliar behaviors, resistance can be anticipated and is legitimate.
- Students have more chance of successfully adopting a less-used learning behavior if they have performance criteria to guide them.

Motivation

Adopting deep approaches to learning, using multiple intelligences, and drawing on learning behaviors that might not be instinctive, all imply that learners have enough motivation to try things that are unfamiliar, are often difficult, and which often put their self-esteem at risk. In exploring the motivational features of student learning environments, we draw upon the book edited by Bess (1997) which explores the interplay between motivation and faculty's attempts to teach well. The frameworks contained in the book apply as much to students as to faculty, although some translation work has to be done.

We can speak of two main forms of motivation, extrinsic and intrinsic. Extrinsic motivation is essentially where we do things for the rewards they bring, or to avoid penalties for not doing them. It is the rewards and punishments that motivate us, not doing the thing itself. Intrinsic motivation is choosing to do something for its own sake, which means that we enjoy it. Activities that we choose, that are challenging (but not excessively so), that allow freedom for self-expression, that provide meaningful feedback, and that are interesting, so that we might experience the joy of doing well, or "flow," as it has been called, are activities that are likely to be undertaken through intrinsic motivation.

In general, intrinsic motivation is better, not least because it avoids the stress that so often goes with extrinsic motivation, stress that can impair our performance. That is not to say that extrinsic motivation is invariably bad, not least because some things that we take on for extrinsic reasons, such as jogging as a way to lose weight, can become delightful in themselves. However, intrinsic motivation is less stressful, associated with better performance, and is more durable. It also is associated with attempts to make meaning and to understand, whereas extrinsic motivation can lead to sacrificing understanding, doing whatever is necessary to achieve the reward or avoid the punishment. It can be associated with surface approaches to learning, whereas this is possible but far less likely when the motivation is intrinsic. Lastly, extrinsic motivation reduces a person's sense of self-determination, that is of having choice and autonomy. That is important, given the conclusion by three contributors to Bess' book that "...when self-determined, people perform better on complex tasks..., process information more flexibly..., are more satisfied at work..., learn better..., are more creative..., persist more..., and achieve better" (Deci, Kasser & Ryan, 1997, p. 59).

This raises the question of why people should choose to take on a task. This choice involves a probably subconscious calculation of whether we can do it. Here, experience will be a guide, and if our experience is of failure, then it is less likely that we will choose to take on this task. However, it is also important to consider how we explain past failures and successes. Table 2.5 illustrates four main ways of explaining success or failure, or "attributions" as they are known.

If we believe that difficulties are caused by factors outside our control (cells 3 and 4), there is little incentive to try again. Some of these attributions have a more profound de-motivating effect than others. Bad luck might change, and the professor for one class is unlikely to be the one who will take the next class. The most corrosive attributions are to negative, personal characteristics that we believe to be beyond change. Students who believe themselves to be stupid will adopt "learned helplessness," and are likely to end up in the avoidant learning style category and to have apathetic approaches to learning. Both are good ways of doing the very important job of preserving self esteem, since what is not done, or that is consciously done poorly cannot damage self-esteem by leading to an

Table 2.5.
Attributions of Success and Failure

	External Factors	Internal Factors
Within our control	1. Availability of materials; access to the library; time.	2. Persistence; commitment; strategy.
Beyond our control	3. Bad luck; the professor hates me; discriminatory practices.	4. Ability (or G!); fixed aspects of personality.

unexpected bad grade. Students who do that can always say that they would have done better had they tried, preserving their self-esteem from the possibility that they might have tried and still done badly. Similarly, where students believe that they haven't the capacity for hard work, the ability to read difficult books, the skill to work fast, or the personality to work well in a group, they can best preserve their self-esteem by not trying. On the other hand, where attributions are to things that are within our control, there is the possibility of doing better, especially if we have feedback or guidance from someone else who shows us how to go about doing better.

That analysis contains some very important points about the student learning environment. It needs to have many opportunities for success, to give learners advice about how to improve, and, above all, avoid things that could freeze learners' failure into a belief that nothing can be done. When talking about poor performance, the best teachers will draw attention to factors that lie in cells 1 and 2 of Figure 2.1, to things that are within the control of the student, indicating how the student might take control to good effect.

Now, to return to the overall motivational estimation of the effort a task requires and the chance of success. Assume that the student does take on the task. There is a calculation, to which we have already alluded, about the amount of effort that is necessary for the desired performance. If the task demands more effort than seems reasonable, then a normal response will be to scale back effort, or to avoid the task entirely. But there is a further issue. Will the performance have a high chance of bringing success of a sort that is valued? This is related to the learner's experiences, to the support available, and to attributions. And all of this converges in a final calculation about the value of successful performance.

The implications for the learning environment of these notes on motivation are that:

- There are good reasons to give students choice, thereby creating more opportunities for intrinsic motivation to operate.
- Interesting material and teaching approaches have learning advantages (intrinsic motivation).

- Tasks should be realistic, in that students should be able to succeed, in their terms, on them. That might be a warning against overloaded courses (some natural science courses "grow content," seldom weeding out old material); it is a signal to give students guidance on doing unfamiliar types of task; and it suggests that it is not a good strategy regularly to set hard tasks to "sort the sheep from the goats."
- It is helpful for students to know and understand the reasons why a task is set, and why teaching and learning take the form that they do. This is important to the calculation of the value of doing a task, as opposed to not doing it, or of doing it in a familiar and inappropriate way.
- Success is best seen in terms of the learner mastering things that were not previously possible. That means that norm-referenced assessment (see Chapter 4) is undesirable and that criterion-referenced grading is vastly preferable.
- Feedback to students is important, especially where it focuses on things that learners can do to improve future performance. Feedback that fosters "learned helplessness" is poisonous to learning.

Happy students

A good learning environment, as described above, should lead to happier students. The main exception is their running into expectations and tasks that are unfamiliar to them. Then the environment becomes seen as hostile, even though the teacher had been trying to make it better for learning, and students' reactions can become critical and difficult. This is often experienced by professors whose courses are different from the other courses in a program (usually because they are innovative courses). It is for this reason that we have been implicitly considering the student learning environment as something that a department fosters throughout a program. It is possible to work within one course to produce a better learning environment, but the greatest impact is the whole program having that aim. If you are improving your course learning environment, and that involves developing features that are distinctive within your department, then four pieces of advice are these:

- Share with the students the reasons why your course is different and tell them what's in it for them.
- Make sure that there is a structure in place to help students cope with new demands: hints in print or on the website; support systems, such as ALSs (see p. 101) or "buddy systems"; and ways of contacting you or TAs.
- Make sure that there are not too many novel features for students to come to grips with in any one part of the course: beware of innovation overload.
- When you meet with the class, spend time trouble shooting and bug hunting.

Our thinking about student learning environments is that making students legitimately happy is an important goal of teaching. There is some justification for this stance in the literature that suggests that happiness has some association with better work, but we do not wish to rest too much weight on that point. Rather, we suggest that, all things being equal, it is morally preferable to try to make students happy than to make them suffer.

So, if you turn back to Table 2.1, you might be able to see why the Downtown Metropolitan learning environment is generally preferable to Pinawa's (not in terms of the plant and resources, though!). Table 2.6 (pp. 32-33) contains our mapping of the features of the learning environment on to the topics discussed above.

The creation of favorable learning environments is about thinking systemically, by which we mean that it involves looking at all aspects of the way that we plan for student learning. For example, it involves thinking about what we ask learners to read (many—perhaps most—textbooks encourage surface approaches to learning) and about what we want them to do with what they have read; it involves asking whether reading can be supplemented, or sometimes displaced, by viewing or listening; it is about giving students choice and support; about setting tasks that invoke a range of understandings, skills and qualities; and about aligning a range of learning, teaching and assessment methods so that they reinforce each other. And so on.

Creating good learning environments is, in this sense, about good planning, which is the subject of the next chapter. And it is also about planning in terms of students and of learning. We have already said something about learning and it is easy to assume that the students' part is self-evident. But students are not homogenous and diversity is growing. As access to higher education continues to widen so that more people from groups that have not traditionally been prominent in higher education are increasingly entering (but less often graduating from) higher education, planning in terms of students means planning for diversity. Whatever the common cultural bonds that draw a nation together, there are also powerful cultural currents that swirl together and produce diversities: some of these cultural currents are associated with differences in wealth, disability, urban or rural homes, gender, religion, parental education, race, class, immigration status, substance usage, age, occupational identity, and sexual orientation. An illustration of the ways in which cultural assumptions impact on classroom teaching is contained in Box 2.3.

A word of caution is also needed. Better learning environments are associated with different performances than those that are associated with degraded environments. Yet, these are differences on average. Some learners' approaches, motivations, and behaviors will not change, and in other cases the changes might be small and inconsistent. Furthermore, there can be problems if faculty members are judged by how well students do on traditional measures of academic achieve-

Table 2. 6.
Theoretical Underpinnings of the Cultural Aspects of Downtown Metropolitan University's Student Learning Environment

Aspect of Learning Environment	Downtown Metropolitan	Link with Learning Theories
Institutional support for teaching	Committed to teaching, although more could be done	Faculty motivation–valuing attention to teaching
Faculty orientation to teaching	Committed to it	Necessary to teach with enthusiasm and sensitivity to students
View of teaching	Students construct their own understandings	Supportive of deep approaches to learning
Faculty disposition to students	Friendly and accessible	Helps to create a climate where students will take risks (deep learning) and get good feedback
Teaching goals	Content mastery plus development of general skills and qualities	A major implication of theories of multiple intelligences and diverse learning behaviors is that there ought to be variety in pedagogic and assessment practice.
Teaching methods	Varied	
Learning methods	Varied learning methods embedded in courses	
Range of learning styles supported	Wide	
Range of intelligences supported	Student choice means that there is some scope to select courses and tasks matching the strongest intelligence	
Evaluation	A mix of methods used to foster the desired mix of learning outcomes	As above. Also necessary for deep learning approaches and for intrinsic motivation.
Student attitude to evaluation	A chore, but it can be interesting and involve collaboration with others	Collaboration is useful as an aid to deep approaches and suits some intelligences and learning behaviors

Table 2. 6 (cont.)
Theoretical Underpinnings of the Cultural Aspects of Downtown Metropolitan University's Student Learning Environment

Aspect of Learning Environment	Downtown Metropolitan	Link with Learning Theories
Clarity of evaluation criteria (hence of course and program goals)	High	Motivation
Feedback to students	Points to ways of improving work for the next time	Motivation and supporting deep approaches to learning
Learning approaches favored by this climate	Deep	Usually preferred over surface approaches. Might not be as good as strategic, but that approach assumes mastery of deep approach
Favored motivation in this student learning environment	Intrinsic (extrinsic for those who just want to make the grade).	Intrinsic motivation generally seen to be more efficient and more effective.

ment. Students working in what we have seen as good learning environments should, on average, develop in ways that are not always measured by traditional forms of grading. Furthermore, because these environments are more demanding, since students are expected to master the material and to consolidate less-familiar ways of working, then there can be some decline in performance on traditional measures of academic achievement. In this case, the issue becomes one of the purposes and goals of the course, program, and university education in general. The environments we favor will tend to produce students who differ from those emerging from impoverished environments.

So, the starting point in course planning is some degree of assurance about what it is that the program is designed to do and to value. In many cases, those goals will require that the learning environment be developed on the lines of that at Downtown Metropolitan University. As a planning issue, we carry the development of good student learning environments into the next chapter.

2.3. Cultural Variations and Learning

Social customs, learning styles, repertoires of behavior and expectations of self are all constructs that differ to greater or lesser degrees in different cultural currents.

In some cultures it's seen as impolite to look directly into the teacher's eyes, which can be disconcerting and frustrating for people who are accustomed to the opposite. Some cultures have a "role of silence." The idea behind this is to hide your potential mistakes and save face rather than risk embarrassment. Humility and modesty can also require silence for fear that otherwise you might show off your knowledge in front of others. Teachers who are unaware of different cultural norms could presume that students who seem to sit in stony silence might not be understanding the material—or that they are indifferent to it and unappreciative. These same students might also feel uncomfortable about accepting well meaning compliments because for them it is not acceptable to think one person is "better" than the other and humility is a great virtue.

Again, we expect students to speak up, to respond immediately to questions, and not take their time ("we have a lot of material to cover, you know"), but in some cultures that is not acceptable either. It is felt that it's irresponsible—disrespectful almost—to answer immediately. An answer needs to be a thoughtful answer and that in itself takes time.

Nor are all students familiar with the ways in which we commonly break complete and complex topics into pieces—a fragment here-a fragment there with selected-response test questions to be done under tight time restrictions.

Finally, it helps to remember that a rapid rate of speech for students can be problematic. In some cases, rapid speech is regarded as not thoughtful. In other cases, English is a second language, and even where it is the first tongue it might be a very different sort of English from our well-rounded, extended sentences with their rich vocabulary, refined participles and interlocking subordinate clauses.

And we have not even mentioned reading and writing as academic practices that have a variety of culturally-set meanings, let alone critical perspectives that see cultural hostility embedded in academic life—perhaps in the form of the pervasive discourse of capitalist patriarchy masquerading as normality.

3. The Course Syllabus: Planning for Practice

Preview

Good planning is an important step towards better teaching. When we plan for better practice we bind ourselves to trying to make a go of it, so we make a more serious commitment than if we decide to improvise improvements during the year. When planning is clear and full, then improvements can be mindfully designed.

A result is documents such as the course syllabus and assessment plan (Chapter 4) that tell students exactly what is intended and what will be expected of them. It is important that they are not left in the dark. That implies writing in a full and accessible style.

Figure 3.2 suggests that planning does not have to follow the sequence you might have expected. Begin anywhere and go anywhere, as long as all the bases get covered in the end. That recognizes that course learning outcomes are often not the starting point but emerge during the planning process.

Boxes 3.1 and 3.4 provide templates to use in course planning.

Box 3.5 contains hints on giving your paper-based course an information and communications technology (ICT) make-over.

Planning Processes

Courses can take a variety of forms and operate under a variety of constraints, so any advice on planning is given in the knowledge that changes will have to be made to accommodate the circumstances in which planning actually happens. Figure 3.1 (p. 36) contrasts what people think ought to happen with research findings about the way that schoolteachers really do plan.

Following the themes of Chapter 2, we also suggest that good planning involves planning for a diversity of learning, teaching and assessment activities; that students should be given as much choice as possible; and that depth is preferred to breadth of coverage.

Ideally, planning should be collaborative. We have three things in mind here. The first is that a course is often a development of something that has run in the past. In that case, it is a good idea to draw upon student evaluations when plan-

Figure 3.1
Two Assumptions About Course Planning Processes

Presumed Rational Planning Sequence   *Planning Sequence Identified by Researchers*

Sequence of Objectives   Content Sequencing
| |
Content   Techniques/Lessons that Have Worked in the Past
| |
Teaching Methods   Proven Assessment Methods
| |
Assessment (Evaluation) Methods   Objectives

ning. Better still, convene a focus group of students who have taken the course and ask for their suggestions about strengthening it. Secondly, there is value in sharing a draft of the course with colleagues. It does not matter if they are not expert in your subject specialization. What matters is that they can comment on the goals, learning, teaching and assessment strategies, as well as commenting on the quality of advice to students. Thirdly, course planning should be collaborative in the sense of being sensitive to the structure of the program within which it is being provided. We know that there are programs whose goals are principally content coverage and where courses are offered on a "pick and mix" basis. There are also programs that are designed so that, over four years, students progressively develop understandings, skills and qualities through engagement with a carefully-conceived sequence of courses and electives. In those cases, the design of one course should involve a "virtual collaboration" with the design of the program as a whole. Currently, this approach is much in favor in official thinking in Britain.

The final point in this introduction is that we suggest that course planning and the production of a handbook, web page, or syllabus for the students are activities that are best done simultaneously. We see the course syllabus as an extended and public version of the course plan, and will tend to refer to it rather than to plans that are made for other purposes, such as for submission to course approval committees.

The Course Syllabus

The course syllabus is a course plan that is shared with students.

One of us remembers being advised, back in 1969, to keep the course plan brief: "don't commit yourself to anything you don't have to!" was the advice of an elderly, well-respected colleague.

How many young faculty members have been so advised? We know of quite a few. Keeping a course outline short; providing the minimum of information required by department, faculty or university regulations provides some flexibility, but allows the faculty member to avoid commitment, and leaves the students guessing. We would like to advise all faculty to create commitment. Students will be better informed about the course right from the beginning, the likelihood of dispute over marks using schedule problems as a reason will decrease, but most important, commitment to the course in an "up front" form by the teacher is an essential first step to teaching a successful course.

In her very useful book on writing a course syllabus, Judith Grunert (1997) gives 16 functions of the course syllabus. They are listed in Box 3.1. Some of the sixteen are not what you would necessarily expect to find in a course syllabus, some of them (we identify numbers 3, 4, 6, 7, 10, 11, 12, and 16) are vital, and all of them lie far beyond the philosophy of "don't commit yourself to anything you don't have to!" Above all, the idea of a full course syllabus is important to us because it follows from our belief that people learn best when they know what the aim or goal is, what the "rules of the game" are, and what choices they have. Another value, often overlooked, is that once you have publicly committed yourself to attempting something that itself is a force to encourage you to do it. It is for this reason that there is such interest in the UK in encouraging program planning that has best practice "designed in." The thinking is that, although there will be a slippage from the design in practice, good design will encourage better practice.

3.1: Functions of the course syllabus (Grunert, 1997, pp. 14-19)

1. Establishes an early point of contact and connection between student and instructor
2. Helps set the tone for your course
3. Describes your beliefs about educational purposes
4. Acquaints students with the logistics of the course
5. Contains collected handouts
6. Defines student responsibilities for successful course work
7. Describes active learning
8. Helps students assess their readiness for your course
9. Set the course in the broader context for learning
10. Provides a conceptual framework
11. Describes available learning resources
12. Communicates the role of technology in the course
13. Can expand to provide difficult-to-obtain reading materials
14. Can improve the effectiveness of student note taking
15. Can include material that supports learning outside the classroom
16. Can serve as a learning contract

With those functions in mind, we move to the process of planning a course.

Planning a Course

This section is organized as a commentary on the planning sequence whose main stages are summarized in Figure 3.2. Although this chart has to be in a linear form, it is not necessary to start at point 1. Points 4, 5, or 8 would all be good starting points. The important thing is to ensure all points are covered: the sequence in which that is done is a matter of one's own planning style.

Figure 3.2.
A Course Planning Sequence

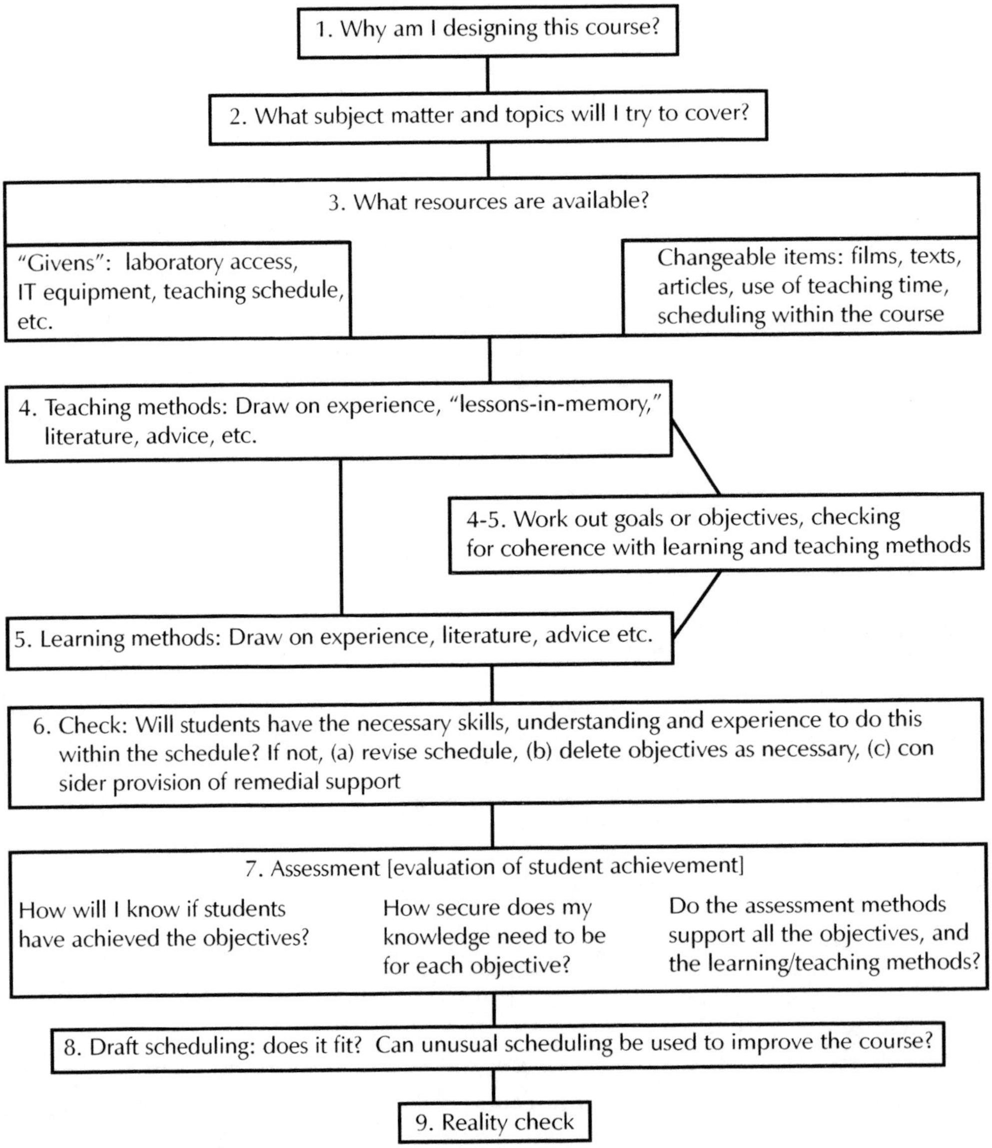

1. Why am I designing this course?

2. What subject matter and topics will I try to cover?

3. What resources are available?

| "Givens": laboratory access, IT equipment, teaching schedule, etc. | | Changeable items: films, texts, articles, use of teaching time, scheduling within the course |

4. Teaching methods: Draw on experience, "lessons-in-memory," literature, advice, etc.

4-5. Work out goals or objectives, checking for coherence with learning and teaching methods

5. Learning methods: Draw on experience, literature, advice etc.

6. Check: Will students have the necessary skills, understanding and experience to do this within the schedule? If not, (a) revise schedule, (b) delete objectives as necessary, (c) consider provision of remedial support

7. Assessment [evaluation of student achievement]

| How will I know if students have achieved the objectives? | How secure does my knowledge need to be for each objective? | Do the assessment methods support all the objectives, and the learning/teaching methods? |

8. Draft scheduling: does it fit? Can unusual scheduling be used to improve the course?

9. Reality check

1. Why Am I Designing This Course?

Because I have to.

It is possible that you have been told to design a course but that you have no great interest in teaching. Equally, you might have to redesign a course in order to improve student evaluations, or to reduce your time commitment. Chapters 4-7 contain suggestions for ways of teaching a conventional, content-focussed course that should lead to greater student appreciation. Point 8, below, contains some suggestions for reducing your time commitment and there are more ideas in Boxes 7.7 and 8.8.

To improve student learning of the subject matter.

In this case, try to build the following into your course design:

- Combine sessions where you survey the territory with others that allow for a few selected topics to be pursued in depth.
- Build a variety of learning, teaching, and assessment activities into your plan.
- As far as you can, give students a choice of activities.

To combine subject matter learning with the development of skills and qualities

The same principles apply, and it is also necessary to have a view of the following:

- The skills and qualities that you wish to foster (see also Table 1.1).
- What you would regard as evidence of achievement in your course in these skills and qualities.
- The balance between skill development and subject matter learning that you will find acceptable. Which is going to be the more important?

It will then be important, especially at points 4, 5, and 7, to check that the learning, teaching and assessment activities will give students sufficient chance to progress in these skills and qualities. Likewise, an estimate of what they will probably bring to the course (point 6) will be necessary in order to decide how much weight will need to be put on methods designed to promote those skills and qualities. Finally, be rigorous in the "reality check" (point 9); skills and qualities often need more attention than might have been assumed in the initial planning, especially if they have not received attention in colleagues' courses as well.

2. What Subject Matter and Topics Will I Try to Cover?

The biggest single mistake here is to try to cover too much material. Question 7 in Chapter 9 concerns a Physics course, because teachers of natural science subjects seem to find this issue a particularly vexing one. Whatever the subject though, overloading the content coverage is a recipe for surface approaches to learning. The best way of avoiding this pitfall is to adopt the maxim that a secure grasp of concepts and of the structure of the topic allows learners to add information as they need it. Key concepts, then, have more power than does information. Information without the key concepts can be sterile trivia. Where concepts and principles are grasped, detail and fresh topics can be added.

If the overview-and-depth method is used to organize the subject matter, it makes sense to choose the most interesting material for the depth studies, bearing in mind its level of difficulty and the available resources. For example, O'Connell-Davidson and Layder (1994) faced with the unenviable task of teaching social science research methods, used a number of case studies of research into sexual behavior and madness to illustrate methodological issues in their text *Methods, Sex and Madness*.

Lastly, and following the principle of explicitness, it is helpful for students to know why they are studying this material. The explanation that you give should also guide your choice of what to cover and of the depth of coverage. For example, if students have to know about cell metabolism in order to do a laboratory research project, the main aim of the course might be, quite legitimately, to ensure that they have a sure and detailed knowledge of simple cell structures and functions. They need to know that this is the aim of the course and that their success will be judged simply on the level of factual knowledge they can demonstrate. Alternatively, cell metabolism might be used to illustrate microbiological research methods, which would imply that comprehensive knowledge of cell structures would be less important than understanding of principles and research methods. The two different purposes imply very different teaching, learning, and assessment activities.

3. What Resources are Available?

In many subjects, great aims founder in the face of resource issues. Laboratories can only be used—and have to be used—at certain times; the only available teaching room is a tiered lecture theatre; there is no ICT equipment in the teaching rooms; or all of the teaching has to be completed in one semester, which severely limits the possibility of using assessment methods that invite learners to present a synthesis of their understanding of the complete course. Sometimes, these constraints are not as compelling as they seem: for example, it is possible to have small group activities and interchange in a tiered lecture theatre (see Chapter 6), although it might take quite a lot of nerve to try it. On the other hand, one of us would like to put a large part of a course on the web, but is deterred because students, especially part-timers, frequently complain about the difficulty of getting web access (see Box 3.6).

Decisions about other resources are critical. Certainly, resources are often in short supply. Ways of coping with that affect the learning outcomes of the course. For instance, a common way of coping with resource shortages is to give students books of readings, or to direct them to buy a text. In both cases, the professor might think that if students are given lectures that outline the main principles related to each topic and are then expected to make their own notes from the text or reader, then they are becoming independent learners. An alternative strategy is to stay with the lectures that outline the main principles related to each topic and to ask students to choose one of those topics and, unaided, to investigate it in some depth. The assessment item might be a summary of the literature, or an annotated bibliography of half-a-dozen key readings. What is important is that the two responses to the same lack of resources have very different learning potential. One encourages skill at writing a précis, but hardly encourages independence, while the other encourages skill at locating information, evaluating, and synthesizing it independently.

As a rule of thumb, we prefer the second approach, which supports more authentic learning. In the same vein, anything that breaks a dependence on course texts and readers is taken to be, at first sight, more valuable than the alternative of relying on them, although good texts designed into good courses can be invaluable.

Choosing content involves checking that it can be scheduled within the time available. This can only be a rough estimate at this stage because it depends on decisions about breadth and depth of coverage, decisions that can be made now, but it also depends on decisions about the teaching, assessment and learning activities, which are decisions that might yet be made.

4. Teaching Activities

Schoolteachers use their experience of teaching when they plan lessons. They often move from identifying content to be covered to imagining ways of teaching the material, even though learning outcomes have often not yet been identified. To do this, they draw on their experience in the form of "lessons in memory." These are recollections of lessons or routines within lessons that have worked well, sometimes with the very content that is to be covered, sometimes with similar material. So, a mini-research exercise, a role play, a piece of extended writing, memories of a demonstration of ICT use, a couple of good presentations and a good discussion topic might be recalled, and become the starting point for planning the teaching activities.

We prefer to think in terms of "teaching activities," rather than of "teaching methods." Our reasoning is that thinking about "teaching methods" might evoke routine thoughts on the lines of "lectures, lab work, tutorials." Thinking about teaching activities helps to direct attention to what might happen under the heading of those labels. We illustrate this in Chapter 5, where we suggest that the word "presentations" be substituted for "lectures" and show something of the range of teaching activities that can take place within a presentation.

This is a sound way of beginning planning, as long as it is no more than the starting point. It makes sense to use activities that have worked well in the past and in which we have confidence. However, there are two obvious dangers with this approach:

- Our repertoire of teaching activities that work is likely to be a selection of those that *could* work. Furthermore, those that spring to mind might be only a selection of those that have worked for us in the past, some of which have got forgotten.
- Especially when we are considering trying to teach new material, or to concentrate on fostering skills and qualities, it is likely that the activities we have used successfully will not be the ones that are the most powerful for these new purposes.

A two-stage response to these problems is:

1. Deliberately look for other ways of making it so that the material, concepts, skills, or qualities are learned. This probably involves making a list that is based upon thinking about what colleagues do; dipping in to the literature on teaching your subject, or on teaching methods in general; and from attending professional development sessions, or from taking advice from faculty development professionals.
2. If there are certain skills or qualities that came to mind at point 1 of your planning, it is worth doing a "thought experiment" to see what sort of learning experiences would be needed in order to give students a chance to practice these skills, display these qualities, or to give evidence of achievement in qualities and skills. Box 3.2 contains an example of this sort of thinking.

3.2 Early thinking about teaching and learning methods to support skills development

A professor has the thought that she would like her new course to help students to write in more varied ways and to learn about working in groups.

Obviously, opportunities for group work need to be provided. She also decides that the writing should concentrate on students writing short briefing papers that outline points of view and suggest, succinctly, which is preferable and why. She knows that two of the case studies in the outline of the course content relate to earnest debates in the subject. In the past, she has covered these topics through presentations that have laid out the different positions and suggested her opinions.

Group discussion of these topics would offer an alternative way of getting to grips with the debate. However, she realizes that the discussion is likely to be more productive if she can

---

ensure that the range of views represented in discussion is fully prepared in advance. She adopts the following strategy.

In week 5 she gives a lecture on one of the cases that identifies the reasons why the topic has proved contentious, and which sets out the principal positions that have been adopted by different commentators. Lectures are then suspended for a week. In this time, each student is assigned one of the positions in the debate, given a list of key readings and suggestions for ways of finding other references, and instructed to prepare a 500-word summary of that position. Each summary should (a) explain the position, (b) describe the main evidence and arguments that support the position, (c) indicate the main problems with the position, and (d) offer a brief view of the credibility of the position. These summaries are made available to the other students in each task group a day before the next class meeting.

Students get together in their groups in that class meeting. Each student briefly presents the positions that they had prepared. General discussion follows, with one student chairing the discussion, while also participating, in order to ensure that everyone contributes and that no one dominates the discussion. Groups are told, if possible, to reach agreement on the issue, preferably without using the formula that the answer is "a bit of this and a bit of that."

Students then write a 500-word paper summarizing their own thinking in the light of the group discussion. They are encouraged to circulate drafts to each other by E-mail. These summaries are submitted to the lecturer in electronic form. She produces a digest of the papers that represent each position and makes the digest available to the whole class.

She sees that this approach means that a topic that she would have previously covered in one week will now take two and involves two substantial assignments. At that point she reexamines her thinking about the content to be covered in the course. Her question is whether this method has enough advantages for it to be retained at the price of having to cut two lectures from her draft schedule of content coverage. She believes that if she decides to retain this teaching routine, then she will need to make sure that students can earn marks that properly reward their input.

As possible teaching activities are identified, it will become obvious that there are skills and qualities associated with some of them that could become key course goals. In other words, this is a model of possible goals emerging as thinking develops about how to teach the course. We have more to say about identifying goals in point 4-5, below and Box 4.3 is also relevant. Here, we interject two cautionary points:

1. Courses should not have too many goals or planned learning outcomes. Three is a good number, five is pushing the limits of manageability.
2. If one of the possible learning outcomes involves students engaging with a new skill, or using a quality that has not been tapped earlier in the program, allow more time to introduce it, expect students to take longer than expected to use it, and ensure that it is used repeatedly (say, three times) in the course. In such cases, you might wish to reduce the number of intended learning outcomes to allow sufficient attention to be given to this new goal. Plan the teaching activities to allow depth of exposure of the new skill or quality.

Teaching activities are likely to be revisited as decisions about learning, assessment and scheduling emerge. If possible, try to preserve a variety of activities, acting on the principle that variety is generally attractive to students.

Lastly, at this point one of us begins a draft list of teaching principles for the course. For course 2232 it is a list of seven things to keep in mind when teaching this course, an *aide memoire*. It includes, "Have Bach playing as students enter the room"; "This course depends on me giving quick feedback on assignments; make this a priority in planning my schedule"; "Force myself to work around mini-lectures of 15 minutes plus activities"; in tutorials, chair, don't dominate." For 4863, one of the points is, "this is likely to be a very mixed group. Some know a lot about the concepts, others don't understand what a criterion is, let alone what criteria-referenced assessment is."

5. Learning Methods

Learning activities can be divided into two broad groups: those that are not graded and those that are (low stakes and high stakes assessment). In some courses and in some universities, it is usual to grade students every week. Elsewhere, the pattern might be to grade on the basis of a couple of substantial tasks and an examination. That is not to say that students do less work in the second case, for they might do a great deal of seminar preparation, but it is work that is not graded by the tutor. Some people fear that if there are too many ungraded activities, then students will not do the work. We have three answers to that fear:

- Students are less likely to do these activities if they are not persuaded of their value. Some teachers say that examination questions will be based on these activities, rather than on treatments of the material in lectures.
- Peer pressure can be an important inducement to do the work. If students have to contribute their preparation work to a group or action learning set activity, then there is peer pressure for them to do the work.
- Teachers can make informal checks to see if work has been done. These checks include seeing whether everyone has brought notes to a session, asking people to describe what they found, or to talk about problems or issues that they encountered.

Strategies for identifying possible learning activities are the same as those for identifying teaching activities. There is a place for activities that have students adding information to a framework that was introduced in a presentation, but it is generally better to set them questions that require some thought. For example, a learning task that involves analysis, critical thinking, synthesis (drawing together material from several sources), or evaluation, necessarily involves collecting information, but also prompts students to use deep approaches to make sense of that information.

As with teaching activities, thinking about learning activities can suggest further, possible aims for the course. For example, if a possible learning activity involved students searching the web to tune in to discussion groups concerned with occupational health hazards in the grain farming industry, then it would be worth considering whether a course aim might be "to provide practice in complex web searches." In that case, as we show in point 6, it would also be important to think about provision for those few students who are not web-literate. The cost of doing that might deter the teacher, who would then consider alternative activities to engage with the same debates about occupational health hazards.

Checking that the selection of activities is realistic within the constraints of the schedule needs to be done, roughly, at this point. It is important to keep in mind that we will tend to underestimate the time a task will take and forget that if students feel that they have too much to do, then they will often adopt coping strategies and surface approaches to learning. In some universities, courses are planned in terms of student learning hours (SLHs). So a Junior Year course might be allocated 270 student learning hours. This time should include the hours students spend being taught, face-to-face, time being examined (including revision time and examinations), and time on other learning activities, including reading. Although it is not easy to get used to planning a course in terms of SLHs, it does have the great advantage of forcing teachers to estimate the time that students are likely to spend on various activities and to offer those estimates for public comment.

4-5. Work Out Goals or Objectives

Goals emerge throughout course planning, so putting them here in the sequence is somewhat arbitrary. We have suggested that goals should be relatively few in number. It is important to check that those that you select are supported by the teaching and learning activities that you have envisaged. Goals that are not should be discarded, or the activities should be revised.

The form in which goals are expressed varies according to local custom (see also Box 4.3). Some people talk of learning outcomes, others of objectives. Behind both phrases is the idea that it is helpful to everyone to express the goals in a way that is clear and detailed enough to help you—and the students—to see what achievement of the goal would look like. So, "use the web to locate information" is helpful, if rather vague, whereas "use the web to locate two discussion groups on occupational health hazards, and post contributions to both" is much more helpful. In spelling out the learning outcome this way, you have indicated the way that performance will be assessed and success judged.

6. Check.

All statements about goals, choices of learning and teaching activities are based on implicit assumptions about what students will already know and be able

---

to do, and about how quickly and easily they will be able to do it. Frequently, we overestimate students' existing competencies, and we also tend to forget that there will be those who do not meet the expectations that are implicit in our course design. This check really involves wondering what is to be done when there are students who do not come up to these expectations. Possible responses include the following:

1. Abandon the goal in its present form because it is too ambitious for these students.
2. Take the line that some will fail in all courses and that is not your problem.
3. Have students work, as far as possible, in groups, so that those who can help those who cannot.
4. Provide support sessions to bring those students who have difficulties up to speed.

Our preference is for option 3, followed by 1 and 4 (which we rank equally). Response #2 is legitimate, but is most legitimate when other responses have been considered and rejected.

7. Assessing Student Achievement

There is a view that the best place to begin course planning is with the assessment activities. Decide what it is that you wish students to demonstrate and then devise a course accordingly. The organization of this book, with assessment coming before teaching methods, suggests that we have a lot of time for that view. The reason for not adopting it in this account is that faculty often find it hard to think creatively about assessment because they get mired in questions about reliability, accountability, and litigation and believe that everything that is graded has to be graded by the professor and carry a mark that could be sustained in a court of law. We see this as a misunderstanding of the purposes and scope of assessment. At the same time, we recognize its prevalence and respond by not advising that course planning begin with assessment matters.

The most important thing about considering assessment when planning a course is the idea of "consequent validity." In essence, this means that what is assessed is what gets learned: the course becomes defined by what is going to be assessed. Aspects of the course that do not contribute to the assessment process will be ignored or marginalized as students seek to get the best deal in a performance/grade exchange.

The main principle, then, is that if something is important enough to be named as a course goal, then students should have assessments that require them to show their achievement on it. In England, auditors examining the quality of courses and programs are required to see if there is a good fit between the goals, teaching and learning activities, and assessment methods. In a quality course, there is a good match between them.

We recognize, though, that some achievements cannot be assessed reliably enough for it to be fair to award a grade that contributes to the overall course grade. Moreover, some achievements are best subject to self- or peer-assessment, and many faculty would not wish to see those assessments contribute to overall course grades. Recognizing these problems, and in anticipation of Chapter 4, the recommendation here is that a check be made to see that each goal has a fair amount of assessed work associated with it, irrespective of whether that assessment contributes to the final course grade. Assessment plans (Boxes 4.1 and 4.15) should make it clear if this is likely to happen. If they show that a goal is being marginalized, it is important to ask whether it is appropriate for that goal to stand.

8. Draft Scheduling.

We have already suggested that thought should be given to whether the plans will fit the schedule. The reason for making it a separate point here, is to emphasize that calculations about whether the course will fit the available time cannot be made until the assessment arrangements have been pencilled in.

This calculation should obviously be done from the students' perspective, asking whether it is a realistic work schedule for them. However, it is also important to inquire whether it is a realistic schedule for you. There is a good chance that it will be too ambitious: Boxes 7.7 and 8.8 suggest ways of reducing time commitments.

9. Reality check

Will this really work?

The Structure of the Course Syllabus

Style

You might imagine that you are creating a book proposal for the potential publisher. You would want to be sure that you hit all the buttons. Everything about the book that is distinctive, attractive, and saleable would be emphasized. You would want the publisher to go away from the meeting with a sound understanding of what you will produce, and a written outline that gives him, or her, plenty of information to guide him or her to a positive decision.

A student is not much different from the publisher. He or she wants to be stimulated to do a course, and wants to be aware of everything possible about the conduct of the course, deadlines, standards, structure, and so on. We suggest four things to have in mind when writing the course syllabus.

1. *Open style*: Use attractive, friendly language which says that you are approachable and will teach without bias or prejudice: language which conveys some of the excitement you feel your for your subject. You might include illustrations, cartoons, and real-life examples: all of these will improve an outline. Box 3.3 contrasts traditional and friendlier ways of describing parts of a course.

3.3. Two Ways of Writing a Course Syllabus.	
Conventional Style	*Preferred Style*
This course will examine coastal processes, particularly those associated with waves, and review the landforms and sediments found along coastlines.	Everyone has some idea of the strength of waves as they impact on a coastline. We will analyze how waves and other coastal processes cause the development of spectacular land forms from great bedrock cliffs to idyllic beaches, and coastal sediments from massive boulders to fine white sand.
Classes are compulsory. Absences must be explained by means of a doctor's note or other note. Makeup tests or essays will be required if you miss mini-tests or poster sessions.	In this type of course, attendance is very important: discipline yourself to turn up for every class. If, for some reason such as illness or a family problem, you are unable to attend a mini-test or participate in a poster session, please E-mail me. I will normally require a doctor's note, or other note and where possible I will assign you a makeup test or equivalent work. Equivalent work, when the makeup test is not possible, will usually be an essay on the topic that I assign. The essay will be two pages of typed text plus maps and/or diagrams, unless otherwise specified.

2. *Add more:* Language that is highly condensed with abundant information collapsed into short passages is inappropriate in the course outline. All the major points you want to make should be clearly evident: several sentences with a major piece of information in each are preferable to one sentence with several tightly-woven pieces of information in it. Make sure that all the important course events and topics are described. It is especially useful if you present a schedule for the course that indicates what will be done on each meeting of the class. If this is in tabular form then you could also include the due dates in the list, even though you might have mentioned them elsewhere

under the heading on tests or assignments. The schedule is best if it appears on a single page.

3. *Cover the bases:* You must try to anticipate problems before they occur and indicate in clear language that you are flexible and that your flexibility should not be mistaken for laxity. Thus it is often a good idea to provide examples of how you will deal with problems. Box 3.3 gives an example of how the problem of absence could be treated. This will convey that you know what you are doing and have a clear plan for dealing with problems. This will help students understand the limits to their behavior and will save a lot of approaches after class asking, for example, "What happens when the football team is playing away?"; or, "Can I accept a free ticket for a week in Hawaii midway through the course?"

4. *Be helpful:* For instance, in the outline for a large class it is useful to say that even if some people think that being in a large class is not a good experience, you think it can be. And then explain why you think that. Again, if you don't want them to use derivative sources in a term paper, tell them why, in your opinion, such sources are not as valuable in academic terms as are original sources.

In Box 3.4 is a list of the main section headings that might be used in a course syllabus.

3.4. Suggested Contents of a Course Syllabus

Mundane details

1. Course number and title
2. Your name and those of other instructors and seminar leaders involved
3. Schedule of meetings, presentations, seminars, tutorials, labs, etc.
4. Groups, sections, and rooms
5. How students might contact you: telephone, E-mail, office number, times available for consultation

The heart of the matter

6. Purpose of the course—see pp. 37-39, above
7. Course objectives and their value
8. Course content, perhaps set out week-by-week, indicating what the professor will cover and how, and what the learners will do, singly or in groups.
9. Learning and teaching activities (and an explanation of why these activities have been chosen—what's in it for the learner?)
10. Advice on learning resources (and perhaps on learning and study strategies as well)
11. How student performance will be evaluated (again, it's important to explain why any unusual evaluation activities are being used) and the schedule for evaluation (date of tests, due dates for assignments, etc.)
12. How you will handle weakness in assignment, absence from classes, tests, etc.
13. The marking scheme used, rubrics, or criteria applied, and their relationship to university transcript terms and standards.

Giving Your Course an ICT Make-over

In well-tuned teaching, courses are regularly given make-overs: sometimes to take on board new books and journal articles, sometimes because the field has shifted so much that the course has become something of an academic backwater, sometimes because we have become enthusiastic about a better way of teaching or organizing learning, and often because developments in ICT make it possible to work in ways that once were not feasible.

In most subjects and areas it is convenient to have students using information and communications technology, since it gives access to sources and resources that would otherwise be unavailable, whether through remote sensing, bibliographic searches, virtual field stations, web searches, on-line conferencing, virtual field trips, interrogation of expert systems or plain, simple E-mail. In other cases it is access to games, simulations, data management and productivity tools that is more important. ICT strongly supports good academic practice.

A more calculating reason is that students will compete in employment markets that want and expect new hires to have ICT skills. For higher education to contribute to this it is not generally necessary to produce certificates of student achievement, not least because these would date very rapidly. It is, though, important that students should have experience of running appropriate ICT software in complex inquiries and that they are able to draw on those experiences when presenting themselves as ICT-literate people. Furthermore, many of these ICT applications support independent and self-directed learning. Again, the ability to work unsupervised, to take initiative, to manage complex inquiries—to be self-directed—is a valued attribute of new hires. Lastly, ICT also supports interactive learning, which is also valued by employers (see Chapter 6).

So, courses that have ICT use embedded in them have attractions that others do not, even if they cover similar ground. Although it would be best if complete degree programs were planned to give a range of ICT experiences, there is a lot that can be done to give individual courses an ICT make-over. Box 3.5 has suggestions.

Starting as You Planned to Go On

This section finishes with a story that, we think, shows the effect of a lack of planning or of bad planning. It is hard for us to imagine that anyone who had planned a course in the ways that we, or Judith Grunert (1997), have suggested could fail to use the first session to really make an impact. Equally, the story in Box 3.6 is a reminder that good planning is only one part of fine tuning your teaching practices.

3.5. Suggestions for Increasing the Presence of ICT in Your Course

- Routinely give references to web sites, require students to use the web to get a comparative perspective by find comparable data from another country, communicate by E-mail, not by paper notices, and give feedback electronically.
- Set homework tasks that require students to search on-line databases and to select the best five or six matches that they make (Locate three journal papers that would give a good update on [a topic] and be ready to say justify your choice of these three).
- Set homework that requires students to summarize researchers' conclusions about a limited topic—for example, about the effect of (a drug) on the treatment of (a medical condition).
- Set up a class bulletin board, Internet conference or user group on which you and the students post questions and academic notes. Some faculty give course credit for student contributions or make contribution a course requirement.
- In some subjects it is possible to buy computer-based tests of core material which students can use for on-demand self-diagnosis purposes. These programs often have a coaching and drill routine built in, so that students can become practiced in dealing with points of Spanish grammar, for instance. Some teachers will not let students take a course assessment before they have submitted a print out showing a high score on such a test of basic information. Other teachers have established their own, customized question banks.
- Many subjects have self-tuition packages, simulations and games that can support learning of core material and displace didactic teaching. This can save a lot of class time.
- In many subjects a good assignment is to have students set up a piece of commercial soft ware to run data in a particular situation and then to grade them on their use of the package to deal with fresh data that you provide. For example, an accountancy course is examined by a three-hour exercise in which students load the accounting package that they have spent several weeks customizing to analyze a small business's figures and then have to use it to work on problems relating to a new set of accounts that are given to them in the exami nation room.
- Put the course on the web. This is in many ways an attractive option, especially with software such as WebCT to support it. Students can get the presentations on-line, do their assignments and get feedback electronically, work with each other and get peer-review through ICT and follow links to other promising sites and gateways. Since this can be done in their own time and at their own pace, and because the information stays put, rather than flying past as it does in a presentation, there are also advantages of convenience. But, this is not to everyone's taste, some students appreciate the greater face-to-face contact of traditional classes, and it can be very time-consuming to get a course on the web, since a *good* site is more than a set of lecture notes that has been cast into the ether. We don't want to be discouraging and we do want to say that building a good site is a big task and that the only sure outcome of hours spent on your first academic site is that you will find all sorts of ways in which it needs to be improved and redesigned.

3.6. Poor Planning in Action

The professor walks in to the room five minutes late, the first day of classes. Without engaging anyone in the class he walks around the seats distributing his one page course outline. There are still students entering, asking if this is the right class. The professor turns to the blackboard and in bold chalk writes the department name, number and name of the course, and below that his own name. By now almost ten minutes are gone and the flow of students into the room seems to have stopped. The class goes quiet and he starts:

"My name is Dr. John Martin and this is history 2200, l'Ancien Régime: France before the French revolution. You all have a course outline that details the progress of the course, the form of evaluations, the text book that you should buy, and how to contact me. Are there any questions?"

"Is there a final exam?" calls a student from the back.

"Yes, it is also detailed in the outline. Anything else?"

No one speaks up. Dr. Martin picks up the remaining outlines, blocks them together on the front desk, looking around and smiling at the students for the first time.

"Right, then. I will look forward to seeing you on Wednesday at 10 when we will begin by looking at our first topic: pre-Revolutionary French culture."

With that he walks out, pausing only to give a course outline to a student who arrives just as he reaches the door.

"Class begins at 10!" he says, and leaves briskly.

We asked students in a North American University if they had any similar experiences. Twenty eight per cent of the 938 classes taken by the students had begun, more or less, in this way. In other words, something like a quarter of the courses taken by these students were so inefficiently, or poorly planned that in the first lecture as much as 80 per cent of the allocated contact time was discarded by the professor. Moreover, the opportunity to make an impact and to orient students to the course was lost.

4. Assessment

Preview

It is vital to distinguish between low stakes assessment of student learning (which has the formative aim of giving feedback for improvement purposes) and high stakes assessment (which has the summative aim of providing marks for grading purposes). High stakes assessment procedures have to be reliable, which means that some valuable learning outcomes do not often get summatively assessed (because they are expensive and hard to assess reliably).

If we want to assess the full range of course learning outcomes, we need to look at low stakes assessment, where reliability is not such a big issue.

If we want to assess the full range of course learning outcomes, we need to use a range of assessment tools.

Low stakes assessment can be to provide you with information to improve your teaching and to provide students with information to improve their learning.

Peer- and self-assessment have great attractions when used for low stakes purposes.

Everyone gains when assessment is based on rubrics or criteria that are known and understood in advance.

Introduction

> … of equal importance in writing a test is not only knowing content material, but also my peace of mind. I take time to calm myself, relax, possibly to meditate. I reinforce the concept of self by reminding myself that I have done well to this point and why would I blow this test? The answer of course is the wild card (the professor). The question remains, will the professor include in the exam any material which was vaguely or obscurely raised in class? (Paul, a fourth-year university student)

In Chapter 3 we said that assessment decisions are best made at the time when a course is planned. For many teachers, though, assessment is often an afterthought in instructional planning, and something quickly devised—a couple of selected-response tests maybe, a presentation or two, and perhaps an essay thrown in for good measure—of course that is only if you will have enough time to mark it. It is not surprising, then, if students like Paul see assessment as somehow at odds with learning. This chapter is based on the idea that good assessment is fair assessment that encourages and rewards good learning. It is important because good assessment practices make for better student learning and so they signal that an effective instructor has charge of the class.

In this chapter, "assessment" refers to the assessment of student learning. It includes tests of what individual students understand and can do, out-of-class assignments, and classroom assessment tests (where teachers use rough and ready methods to get an idea of how well *a class* has grasped key instructional points). We revisit the overlapping terminology of assessment in question 8 of Chapter 9.

The Assessment Plan

The assessment plan and tests should be devised before instruction takes place so that you know where to start, what content you are going to address, what to incorporate in instructional activities for the students, and—obviously—how and why you are going to assess student knowledge, skills, and understanding. When assessment is designed up-front like that, it becomes integral to, and aligned with instruction, not something apart from it.

Planned up front, the assessment can be as valuable as a road map; it helps you set your sights on where you are going. In this way it helps you to highlight the points that really matter in a course and so avoid wasting time, testing haphazardly, and testing trivia and bits of content fragments assembled quickly at the last minute. If you have this "big picture" it is easier to share it with students who then have what can be a very useful framework around which to arrange the understandings they develop from your classes. Many learners benefit from seeing how the pieces can fit together and when instructors help them to relate the parts to the "big picture" then better learning tends to follow. In other words, the assessment plan indicates what matters in a course, which is why poor plans can indicate vague, muddled, or content-saturated courses. A sample plan is in Box 4.1, and 4.13 contains details of an examination blueprint.

In this way there are no unpleasant surprises—for students or teacher alike. Students respect fair assessment practice; they like to be tested and graded on what has been taught, and they like to know how their work will be graded—well in advance. Fair assessment also supports good learning, always assuming that the assessment plan really does involve you in finding out how far students have progressed with your course goals and learning outcomes. When they have a good assessment plan as a road map, then they can plan and be prepared for their journey into new knowledge. They know what is coming up and know what to prepare for, and you can rest assured that they will not accuse you of leaving them in the dark, which should remove a common source of complaint in student evaluations.

Over seven years one of us has asked students to say what they wished for in a fair tests of their achievement on course. This baker's dozen is in Box 4.2. Notice that these students are not asking for short and easy tests of marginal facts.

4.1. A Course Assessment Plan

Assessment Item	Who Assesses?	Weighting	Course Goal	Course Goal
Assignment: produce a course reader on a topic of your choice	You complete a self-assessment sheet (formative) & tutor assigns a mark *	13%	Locate information	Evaluate significance
Assignment: investigate a topic of your choice and write a report of your conclusions	You complete a self-assessment sheet (formative) & tutor assigns a mark *	13%	Independent enquiry	Evaluate significance
Assignment: give an oral presentation summarizing the literature on one course theme	Peer comments reviewed by tutor, who assigns the final mark *	13%	Oral communication	
Fortnightly self-administered classroom tests	You do: solution sheets kept in the Faculty Office	. None	Knowledge	
Examination: making notes on three topics from a choice of five	At least two faculty members if possible	18%	Knowledge	
Examination: long essay requiring analysis, critical thinking and evaluation based on deep understanding	At least two faculty members if possible	42%	Critical and analytical thought	Evaluate significance

* The marking criteria for each of these assignments are printed in the course handbook that each student has.

So instead of viewing assessment as that thing that is hurriedly tacked on to the end of the course outline — or worse, as an addendum handed out halfway through the course — plan for it as carefully as you would your resources, instructional strategies, or anything else that you might incorporate. Let students know what your position is on due dates and how you will deal with late submissions, something that we discuss further in question 9 of Chapter 9. Assessment, when dealt with thoughtfully this way, becomes a celebration of learning, not a "gotcha" exercise, which is how many students experience it.

Learning Outcomes and Instructional Objectives

Your course has aims, although it is quite possible that you will not always know for sure what the precise learning outcomes will be. As table 4.1 shows, in some subjects and at some times it is possible to specify exactly what learners should understand or be able to do (and to what level) at the end of the course. In others, learning outcomes have to be fuzzier, while elsewhere it might only be feasible to specify the learning experiences to which students have been exposed.

The general principle holds good though, namely that you should aim to be as clear as possible in telling students (and yourself) what will count as evidence of acceptable performance. For example, you might say that "at the end of this course students will understand Descriptive Statistics." That is so loose that it is awfully hard to measure—how will you know that students actually "understand"? What evidence will you have to have to get a good idea that they do understand? The simple answer is that in this subject you can write a more specific statement of what will count as evidence that they know and understand the stuff well enough. In other words, you need the evidence before you can make a fair judgment about

Table 4.1
Types of Learning Outcomes and Associated Levels of Judgement

Degree of Precision in Specifying Learning Outcome	Common in Subjects/Areas Such as …	Sample Learning Outcome	Level of Judgement Needed to Grade Such Outcomes
Very high (Instructional objectives)	Hard sciences, grammar, content-mastery subjects and purposes in general. The underlying assumptions are that there is knowledge that is valuable, indisputable, and should be memorized.	Be able to describe the x functions of (something). Draw diagram of the main parts of a zygospore, after page 117 of the textbook. List the advantages and disadvantages of questionnaire surveys	Small. Computer marking is normal.
High (Learning or instructional objectives)	Applied science subjects where there is a body of knowledge and procedures that can be applied to a range of broadly-similar situations. Translations from one language to another	Using the materials supplied, construct an x that will do y. Medical diagnosis on the basis of prepared case summaries. Technical task performance. Solving closed problems.	Small when assessed by selected-response questions. Low-inference performance criteria keep it small in other circumstances.
Medium (Learning outcomes)	Humanities and social science subjects (sciences too, sometimes) where tasks call for non-routine judgements that often relate to values, aesthetics, complexity, novel situations and poorly-structured problems.	Evaluation of a rural health care system. Comparison of Jacksonian and Jeffersonian concepts of democracy. Identification of and response to problems in the workplace. Oral presentation of the case for x.	High levels of judgement that can be reduced by clear and full performance criteria that are familiar to students and graders alike.
Low (Learning engagements)	Learning goals that we reckon to be intrinsically useful, such as taking responsibility for own learning, being skilled in team work, taking the initiative, but which cannot be reliably or ethically assessed by faculty. They can be written for any subject.	Students will work in groups/reflect on their own progress and achievements/take responsibility for locating key sources/create a piece of work that is aesthetically pleasing to them/etc.	Very high –disagreements amongst judges will be common, even if performance information is available and judgements can be made ethically.

Chapter 4   **57**

what students know and can do. And both you and the students need to know what sort of evidence you are looking for—you need to know so that you can instruct the students well and they need to know so that they see what it is they need to learn.

Box 4.3 shows how this is presented to students on the Descriptive Statistics course. In that example the students are told the purpose for the assignment. Interestingly enough, students like to know why they are doing an assignment and they buy into it better if you share your purpose with them (providing the purpose warrants it—students abhor "busy work" assignments unless they are well rewarded "bird" tasks). Box 4.5 shows how expectations are shared in a case where it is better to talk of learning outcomes than of learning objectives. For a more in-depth guide on writing and using instructional objectives, see Gronlund's 1995 book, *How to Write and Use Instructional Objectives*.

4.3. Learning Objectives in a Descriptive Statistics Assignment

Purpose: The purpose of this assignment is to have you experience student engagement in learning in the context of descriptive statistics. Too often material such as this is learned by rote for a test instead of learning to understand it for its real-world application. Class time will be available for you to work on this project and I will be available for individual/group help.
General Objective: By completing this assignment you will understand descriptive statistics.
Specific Objective: You will demonstrate your understanding, by applying, and communicating to others what you know and understand about central tendency and variance in a real world situation of your choice.
Data Gathering: Data might be obtained from unlimited sources such as the sports world, medical fields, businesses, research station, entertainment world, agriculture, etc.
Procedure: You might wish to work collaboratively as a pair or in a group, or whichever is the best way for you to demonstrate your knowledge and which will be the most useful, meaningful, and interesting for you. There really is no limit to the number of ways to proceed.
Presentation/Representation of Knowledge: Again there are numerous ways to do this, for example by use of charts, video, photo album, slides, models, "filmstrip," dramatization/role play—as an alderman presenting findings, board chairperson, coach, teacher, principal, superintendent, doctor, dentist, caretaker, etc.

Good assessment practices are about more than being clear about what we take as evidence of student learning. It also means teachers thinking about why they are using selected-response tests, or essay tests, or a performance test. Is one kind better than the other? Maybe—it all depends on the purpose, so let us consider the various purposes of assessment next.

Low Stakes and High Stakes Assessment

"Is this going to be on the test?" is a question that is so familiar that it even made it into an episode of *The Simpsons*, where the instructor mentions that his

---

4.4. Learning outcomes in a Social Science assignment

Each group will produce a report, equivalent to 2000 words per group member, of their investigation which I will grade. There are six questions I ask when grading this item:

1. Is there a statement of what the problem or issue is and a preview of your conclusion?
2. Is it clear why this is a significant problem?
3. Is there a summary of literature and ideas that are relevant to the issue or problem?
4. What are your findings or conclusions?
5. Why are these findings or conclusions important?
6. Is there any spark or originality about your conclusions?

The following charts illustrate the profile of achievement in terms of these criteria that will usually lead to the award of grades A through D. (Only two charts are shown for space reasons.) The Gray areas show levels of achievement which will be evident but which might not be convincingly demonstrated.

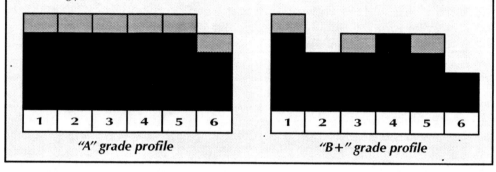

"A" grade profile   "B+" grade profile

wife has just died and Homer asks "Is this going to be on the test?" Told that it will not be, Homer crosses out his scrawled note, "wife has died."

How often have we heard that? Disappointing as it is to hear, it is worth listening to as evidence about what students are really saying about their perception of the purpose of testing and, perhaps more importantly, about their perception of assessment in general.

What students are saying when they ask that question is this: if it is not going to be on the test and for a grade (high stakes assessment), then there is no point in taking it seriously and learning it. Multiple choice or objective tests are the commonest form of "summative assessment"—summative assessment kind of sums up what the students have learned in the whole course. So it makes sense to test the important stuff and not the dull, boring, and inane stuff. Tests should fit your goals and objectives and should be reflect your instructional priorities.

However, there are more purposes for assessment than summative, or end-of-unit testing for grades. Other forms equally important in student learning and assessment, are diagnostic and formative assessment, both of which are low stakes.

Students need to be well aware what the tests are for and should be told why assessment information is being collected and how this will be used. For instance,

---

if students know that the purpose of the assessment is to diagnose strengths and weaknesses (low stakes) rather than to give them a grade, they can be encouraged to reveal weaknesses as well as strengths. But if they know that the purpose is for grading (high stakes), then most will do everything they can to look good on the test and no more.

Low-stakes Assessment: Helping You to Teach Better

Low stakes assessment is where the instructor is not trying to grade students but, instead, to get as much information as possible about what students understand and can do. After gathering this information the teacher analyses it and can then pinpoint the specific weaknesses and strengths and determine ways to address them. The resulting information then informs instruction that in turn, enhances student learning. This sort of assessment is therefore usually done as a pre-assessment at the beginning of a topic or course to find out very specific information about what students know and can do. It can also be done at any other time as a check of progress in a specific area and to see if any students are having difficulty in understanding some of the material. And like the kind of assessment that a medical doctor does when examining a patient's health, diagnostic assessment is done similarly by the teacher—not necessarily looking for weaknesses only, but looking for strengths as well

Sometimes this low-stakes assessment is described as "diagnostic" assessment and sometimes it is called "formative," although the distinction between them appears to be as much a matter of personal taste as of anything else. In both cases the intention is to get information that can be used to improve the instructor's teaching or to give feedback to students to help them improve their learning. It is low stakes assessment because students have nothing to lose by admitting to ignorance but can, as a group, only gain from the better-conceived instruction that should come once the teacher has responded to the evidence of this formative or diagnostic assessment. This section concentrates on low-stakes assessment of groups of students in help you fine tune your teaching to harmonize with their understandings. For more information we recommend Angelo and Cross's Classroom Assessment Techniques which lists 50 well tried methods for exploring what groups of students understand and can do (Angelo & Cross, 1993).

Let us continue to imagine a course that requires some elementary knowledge of statistics, specifically central tendency and variance. Before swinging full force for a couple of hours of teaching this material, it is a good idea to give the students a pretest in elementary descriptive statistics to diagnose their strengths and weaknesses first. That way you can focus on teaching only what is necessary, using at the same time, their strengths as a starting point. By attending to students' needs this way, you are not wasting valuable time, boring the able student, or dashing too fast through the material and leaving the less able confused or frustrated. Because this is diagnostic in nature where you want students to reveal what they do not know as much as what they do know, diagnostic assessment is not used for grading purposes.

When the students know that you are taking the extra effort to carry out diagnostic assessment to help you design your teaching to match their needs, they willingly participate in the low stakes testing knowing that they will not be penalized for revealing their weaknesses. Further, they respect your effort to address their needs this way, and a relationship of respect and trust begins on Day One.

What next? Once you have done a pre-assessment you must carefully analyze the results of the pretest. You might find that perhaps a third of the class that know descriptive statistics "cold," about another third that indicate they have some promise—maybe just forgetting a few concepts here and there—while another third just has no clue. So how should you now proceed? There are a number of possibilities, so let us look at some as examples.

For those students that find the concept "old hat," you could give them the hour or so to get on with next week's reading, catch up on other course work, or just take a break, each of which you should signal is fine with you. Occasionally a few able students might stay to act as coaches. Some seem to like helping their friends and often get greater insights into their own understanding at the same time ("to teach is to learn twice").

You might well notice that those who remain for the remedial teaching seem to feel more comfortable if the able students leave the room. They feel a bit self-conscious about their lack of understanding and are loath to hold the more advanced students up with their elementary questions. How many times have students asked a basic question prefacing it with "this is probably a stupid question, but ...", only to be joined by a chorus of others asking the same question, all visibly relieved to discover they are not alone in the fog?

Sometimes, just a handful of students need the in-depth remedial work. If it is just a few, maybe six or so, you could arrange a tutorial at another time—maybe during a couple of lunch hours. You might be able to link any who cannot make the session up with students who do know the concepts and who could teach it them. (This seems to work just as well and, as we suggested, has benefits for the "teacher" as well as for the "learner.")

Even where you have the kind of course that does not require a pre-assessment because no special conceptual or skill mastery is assumed, it is still a good idea to do a survey of sorts to see where students are coming from—what their background experience is, what their attitude towards the course subject matter is, why they chose the course, and so on—so that you can plan your course around their real-world experience. And even where there is a prerequisite, you usually find a variation of understanding of the pre-required materials, so it is worth the half hour or so up front to find this out sooner, not later, into the course, where you then have to make major adjustments.

In sum, diagnostic assessment can provide information about students' understanding, perceptions and expectations that is used only as a guide to modify your teaching strategies. It also shows a student-centered stance in your work. To repeat: *what you assess, how, and why, says a great deal about you as a teacher.*

Once the course is up and running, some teachers blithely go through the course without having a "reality check." It really is a good idea periodically to invest up to 15 minutes to have the students fill out a short questionnaire to see if we are all more or less on the same page. Some teachers use "exit slips" which can be file cards or slips of paper for the student to write something on at the end of the class. It can be quite open-ended, or you might want it specific—it depends on the purpose. If you do this, you must address what they have written to show that you value their input. If you do not, or do so subtly that they miss it, they will not take this seriously next time and instead of being a "forever better" teacher, you will be forever left in the dark.

Figure 4.1 shows one template for analyzing student responses (and students might be encouraged to write their responses in that form), while Box 4.5 summarizes responses from one class.

Figure 4.1
A 3–2–1 Check for the Analysis of Student Formative Feedback

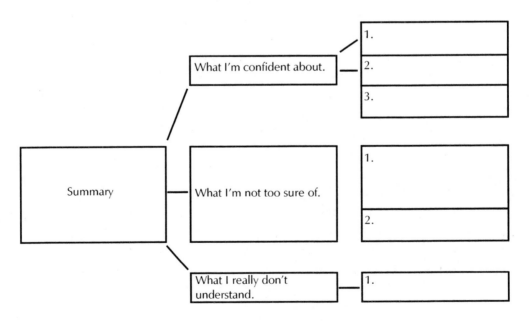

4.5. Results of the 3-2-1 Check

(data taken from the course, *Evaluation of Student Learning* [20 students])

What I know:
* the purposes of formative and summative assessment —9 students
* the importance of fair testing practice —18 students
* the terms, assessment, test, and evaluation —13 students
* the difference between "reliability" and validity —1 student

What I'm not sure about:
* how to develop a blueprint — 5 students
* how to write effective multiple choice questions — 3 students

What I don't have a clue about!
* A few, very specific points from individual students — for example, "How I'm going to find time to do all those blueprints."

Sometimes you do not find out a lot that you did not anticipate anyway, but other times you get real surprises. For example, just when you thought everything is going swimmingly, you might be pulled up short—but just in time before things go further awry. Other times you might be overly concerned about their seeming lack of understanding, only to discover you have been worrying needlessly. You might find out something so simple to remedy such as student frustration that you are not positioning the overheads correctly and some students cannot see.

In the next class be sure to tell students how you are responding to what you found. This might take 10 minutes, but they can see that you are serious about their learning and take a more serious attitude toward class—and your rapport and mutual respect builds from there.

So, in Box 4.5 too many students were *not* saying that they are on top of the purposes of formative and summative assessment and there is a noticeable level of uncertainty about writing blueprints. The teacher needs to say how these more general matters will be tackled. For instance, if a large number of students indicate that they did not understand a concept, you can be sure that there are others in the crowd who are not too sure either but had not said so. It might then be worth going over the purposes of formative and summative assessment with the whole group, even though it might be redundant for some. Alternatively, try to set up peer tutoring on the basis that peers who have the understanding frequently do a better job than you because the student could be more at ease with the peer, and also the peer might go at it a way that you didn't think of. Individual concerns, such as that about time management voiced in Box 4.5, can be gone over during class break or in office hours.

Another approach is to use a pop quiz or surprise tests occasionally as an information gathering exercise and diagnostic tool to see what students understand or recall without preparation. This is a nonthreatening "wake-up call" for both you and the students. However, it is a device that can be used unfairly—without previous warning, to give the students a pop quiz and use their marks in their final grade. This is a questionable teaching and assessment practice because the results will not give you an accurate idea of what the students could do given a reasonable chance and it corrodes the trust that students might have in you.

Low-stakes Assessment: Helping Students to Learn Better

Low stakes assessment activities can also directly help student learning. Exercises such as those we have outlined also serve as student self-assessment activities that require the student to reflect about what he/she knows, understands, and can do. This is extremely important because:

- Self-assessment is an ever-available source of information about how learning might be improved
- Self-assessment is a prerequisite for metacognition—a self awareness about how we learn—and with reflection, both of which are widely seen as keys to good learning (see, for example, Schön, 1983; Costa & Kallick, 1992; Harvey & Knight, 1996).
- The ability to assess and monitor one's own performance is highly valued by employers in a wide range of organizations on both sides of the Atlantic.

Reflective journals also serve as a self-assessment tool. At the end of each lab or class (each week), students write a brief summary of what they have learned and what issues they have before them. This can be shared with the instructor (who will read a sample and use it to inform his/her teaching) or with other students who might be able to offer advice on making good any shortfalls. It is also possible, with care and sensitivity, to grade the quality of reflection manifest in these reflective writings. The criteria should focus on the reflection, not on the quality of the experience or activity that is being reflected upon. For example, a student who wrote a reflection about a class field trip could quite well indicate that she learned little from the trip but has learned a great deal by thinking about why the trip failed and how more could have been gained from it. That is the material to look for, not whether it was a good or bad experience. The important thing for the student is to ask how she could carry out the assignment or activity next time so that improvement can be made. This will often involve her identifying ways in which she could make best use of her strengths and address the weaknesses that are identified by the reflection upon the activity or experience.

To self-assessment can be added peer-assessment, where students give feedback on each other's completed work or comment on draft papers, plans, posters, charts, or other work that will be revised and later be graded. In both cases this feedback is most useful when there are clear criteria or standards that can be dis-

---

cussed and applied to the work. Often these criteria will come from the instructor, although sometimes they are devised by the learners (see Box 4.8, below).

It is easiest to handle self- and peer-assessment when they are done for low stakes purposes and do not contribute to course grades. Where the stakes are low, disclosure is maximized, communication and discussion are encouraged and learning potential is at its greatest There are, though, reports of self- and peer-assessment being used for high stakes purposes, where grades are awarded, although this is illegal in some states. Box 4.6 contains advice for peer-assessment that contributes to course grades.

4.6. Using Peer-Assessment for High Stakes Purposes

Sometimes the instructor is unable to see the work that a student does behind the scenes, especially during group projects and presentations. Done properly, peer-assessment ensures that fair practice is in place rewarding the participating and diligent student. On the other side of the coin it also gives the "easy rider" his or her due, as long as the assessment is done anonymously, with a set of clear criteria in place, and a shared understanding of the purpose of the assessment. *In these circumstances* there is quite a lot of research evidence that the mean peer-assessed mark is close enough to the instructors' marks to be acceptable (see also box 7.8).

The convention is usually that peer assessment is not meant to make or break a student; it is meant to fine tune the final grade, for example, the peer assessment weight should be enough to separate a B from a B+ for example, or be worth about 5%.

It's a good idea to set up the assessment criteria or rubric in class with the students so that they have some ownership; an opportunity to enrich the rubric with things that you might have overlooked; and a realization that you want to be fair in your assessment. If time is short, share with them a draft that you have prepared, discuss and make appropriate changes where applicable. Once finalized, give students a copy to use.

A class identified qualities that they reckoned to be important to use when assessing individuals' contributions to a group project and presentation. Each quality could be assessed at four levels. Examples of the rubrics, criteria or level descriptors are:

Input:
    4 Excellent: The student provides valuable input into the presentation by researching the content and creating a very interesting and meaningful presentation.
    3 Proficient: The student provides reasonably valuable input into the presentation by re searching the content and creating an interesting and meaningful presentation.
    2 Limited: The student provides limited input into the presentation.
    1 Inadequate: The student provides inadequate input into the presentation.

Weight:
    4 Excellent: The student very clearly pulls his/her weight in the group work.
    3 Proficient: The student adequately pulls his/her weight in the group work.
    2 Limited: The student pulls his/her weight in the group work but only to a limited extent.
    1 Inadequate: The student clearly does not pull his/her weight in the group work.

Support:
    4 Excellent: The student strongly supports group peers, by tactfully addressing strengths and weaknesses and by helping the group address those strengths and weaknesses most

---

of the time.

3   Proficient: The student satisfactorily supports group peers, by tactfully addressing strengths and weaknesses and by helping the group address those strengths and weaknesses generally some of the time.

2   Limited: The student's support of group peers is weak

1   Inadequate: The student's support of group peers is inadequate.

Ratings for one student, Denise, were collected and tabulated as shown below.

Name of student	Quality 1 (mean)	Quality 2 (mean)	Quality 3 (mean)	Quality 4 (mean)	Quality 5 (mean)	Total	Mean, Q1-5
Denise	3	2	3	4	4	16	3

If there are any discrepant individual peer evaluations, it is wise to not include that one because it is likely that it does not reflect the student being assessed. For example, if all other students in the group give a student full marks or close to for a student, for example a 3 or 4 on the 4-point scale, but one student in the group gives 2s, it can be more likely a personality clash has interfered with the scoring. Safe practice in these circumstances is to discard any *one* rating that is out of line with the others (see also Box 6.3).

There is far much more to be said about low stakes self- and peer-assessment than we can even hint at here. In addition, the instructor can be involved in low stakes assessments to help student learning. A formative task can be given during the course to let the students know of their progress, and allow them to reflect about their strengths and areas to improve. As Box 4.7 indicates, it should be marked so as to pinpoint strengths (which might need no further attention form the learner) and weaknesses (which should receive attention during the remainder of the term). In conventional grading a student might get 15/20 for an essay but does not know how to improve upon it. An analytical scoring guide reveals areas for development.

There is a case for saying that this analytic approach to grading essays, term papers and other complex work is a good one to use in high stakes assessments as well. The principles behind that position are these:

1. The criteria used should reflect a selection of the course learning objectives/outcomes.
2. The criteria remind the teacher about what is being valued, and therefore contribute to higher levels of reliability and fairness in grading.
3. The criteria give students more information about what to concentrate upon when doing this task: they help learners to learn better.

Students can also usefully devise rubrics or criteria as shown by Box 4.8.

4.7. Essay Analytic Scoring Guide

Name	Title		Date	
Criteria	Possible Marks	Actual Mark	Comments	
Content: accurate, pertinent, convincing, imaginative, perceptive	4			
Development and organization: coherent, unified, logical introduction, development and effective conclusion,	3			
Paragraph development and organization: clear statement of topic, effective development, varied paragraph structures	3			
Point of view/voice: consistent, appropriate in mood and emphasis to purpose and approach	2			
Style: suitable expression, flow, flavor, flair, freshness, interest	2			
Sentence structure: appropriate sentence variety such as contrast, parallelism, balance, repetition, and exclamation	2			
Diction: specific and appropriate vocabulary, imaginative, vivid, precise	2			
Language conventions: correctness of spelling, grammar, punctuation, avoidance of run-on sentences, etc.	2			
TOTAL (20)				
COMMENTS AND SUGGESTIONS:				

4.8. Student-constructed Criteria or Rubrics

This takes some extra class time initially but

> ... it helps enormously to involve students in developing rubrics which help spell out the criteria for different levels of performance ... In the past, the assessment process has been kind of mysterious ... students were "shooting blind." But when students are involved in developing assessment criteria, the [students] know what they have to do to [perform] well—and guess what? They do it. (Charlotte Danielson, cited in Willis, 1996, pp. 1 & 4.)

Procedure

1. Introduce the approach and arrive at a shared understanding of the purpose, e.g., develop a clear scoring guide to assess peer group work fairly (or an oral presentation, poster, etc.).
2. Brainstorm the important attributes in peer group work that a good group member must have or exhibit. So that this doesn't get too cumbersome, try to limit the attributes to about five—for example, "willing to compromise," "does his/her share of work, is respectful to others," "attends group meetings," and "contributes to the group."
3. Through discussing each one, arrive at a shared understanding of what the attribute, for example, "contributes to the group" means.
4. Next, set performance levels. Limit the levels to an even number (4 is best) to avoid central tendency in evaluating.
5. Students then decide on a label for each performance level. For example, a 4 could be "awesome"; 3 could be "almost a master"; 2 could be "getting by"; and 1 could be "not there yet." Alternately, "expert"; "practitioner"; "apprentice;" and "novice."
6. Next, explain the meaning of the highest performance level for each attribute—for example *"significantly* contributes to the group" and arrive at a shared understanding of what *"significantly* contributes" means.
7. It is easier to now go to the lowest level where you identify what performances are not acceptable, e.g., "little to no contribution to the group." Then explain the meanings of the intermediate levels.
8. Review the criteria and fine tune for shared understanding.
9. Assure students that changes can be made during its use, so that no one is at a disadvantage by having it used on them first.

A criterion-referenced approach to assessment gets around a common problem with giving feedback. Frequently, feedback is so detailed and specific to a particular topic that it has no transfer value—it does not help the learner do the next essay, term paper, or whatever. With criterion referencing, though, we see feedback that is given largely in terms of *general* learning outcomes and that does have transfer value. Even high stakes assessment can provide useful feedback for future learning, as long as the feedback is in terms of learning outcomes that are valued on other courses and as long as the feedback actually gets to the students, rather than languishing uncollected and unwanted in the Faculty Office.

In this case, though, the essay is a low stakes task because it provides comments, not grades. Some instructors would say that they do not have the time to do anything except grading. Box 4.9 shows how that objection can be met. It also shows how much easier it is to be adventurous with assessment when the result is not going to be grades. There has been a lot of interest in extending the range of assessment techniques so that the emphasis moves away from awful tests towards "authentic assessment" that is more faithful to complex learning and real-world issues. The problem is that it can be time-consuming, expensive, difficult, and even impossible to have authentic assessments that are reliable and fair enough to provide course grades. A part solution to the problem is to stick with authentic assessment but to use it for low-stakes purposes to give students feedback that they can use to improve their own learning.

4.9. A procedure for the formative, low stakes assessment of essays.

Students are told that it is a course requirement that they will:

1. Write a paper or essay (topic, length etc. to be specified). The paper should be identified by a number, not by the student's name.
2. Complete a schedule (rubric or grading sheet) that assesses their own paper against preset criteria as well as in terms of its key strengths, areas for development. (Again, identified by number.)
3. Read two other papers and for each, complete the same assessment schedule that was used for self-assessment purposes.
4. Meet in groups of three to review each other's papers and to identify no more than three ideas for performance improvement for each learner.

Marks are awarded for completion of each of these four stages but not for the quality of the papers, assessments, or discussions. Experience shows that group processes work powerfully to make this a very good assessment and learning activity.

David Boud's *Enhancing Learning through Self Assessment* and John Cowan's *On Being a Reflective Teacher in Higher Education* are both valuable on low stakes assessment.

High Stakes Assessment: Grading Students

Grading students is a serious business and has to be done to standards that will withstand challenge in law courts: procedures need to be fair and nondiscriminatory and the instruments, tools or methods we use need to be reliable, which is to say that they should produce "objective" or "unbiased" data. Unfortunately one way of gaining greater reliability is to reduce the amount of judgement or inference that is involved in an assessment and to stick to assessing things that are clear cut. In this way high reliability is brought, unwantedly, at the expense of high validity. High validity assessments get at the full range of often-ambitious course goals and learning outcomes. But only some of them, notably knowledge goals, can be assessed reliably and cheaply. Others, such as understanding, can be assessed reliably and at a price, while yet others hardly are reliably assessed. So, high stakes assessment means that a concern for reliability and its price is pervasive.

Summative assessment probably requires the least explanation because it is the one we traditionally use when we think of assessment. It provides grades or scores and is used for a formal evaluation (or a judgment) that occurs at the end of a unit, activity, or course, to determine student achievement and program effectiveness. This is the one that we term as "finals"—the three-hour marathon paper-pencil test that can contain selected-response, short answer, or essay questions. In some cases it might be a performance based-test such as a lab in science, a piano recital in the arts, presentation (see also question 10, Chapter 9), extraction of a tooth in dentistry, or a gymnastic sequence in athletics, and so on.

But because summative assessment matters so much—it is high stakes assessment—we need to be sure that it is fair and that the results are reliable. As we have said, that places some limits on what we can assess summatively and how. It also means that we need to be careful about combining summative and formative purposes in one activity. It is fine to set a high stakes task and then to give students feedback about general points for attention, although if it is an assessment at the end of a course, that will often be a waste of effort since many students don't even pick up their final assignments. The problem comes with setting a formative task, where students should expose weaknesses and uncertainties in order to get the best feedback for learning, and then to use their work for high stakes purposes. There can be ethical problems where low stakes tasks are subsequently used as sources of high stakes data.

There are several ways of getting high reliability in high stakes assessment. One is to set questions that take little judgement to grade and which can even be marked by machines. An alternative is to set more complex and authentic questions but to have a clear marking scale—a holistic scoring guide—that is less complex than the analytic scale shown as Box 4.7. Box 4.10 is an extract from one holistic scoring guide and it can be seen that its relative simplicity helps the grader to see the "big picture" and increases the likelihood of a reliable grading. Values can be assigned to each of these levels and easily translated into marks. Sometimes you might see it called impressionistic scoring because it captures the overall impression.

4.10. A Holistic Essay Scoring Guide

Meets expectations
Content: The student used accurate and pertinent content for the most part. The student was generally quite convincing, perceptive, and showed some good imagination in expressing the content.
Development and organization: The student constructed a reasonably coherent, unified, logical introduction, development and effective conclusion.
Paragraph development and organization: The student expressed a somewhat clear statement

---

of topic, constructed an effective development, and varied paragraph structures well.

Point of view/ voice: The student's writing is usually consistent, appropriate in mood and emphasis to purpose and approach.

Style: The student's writing has reasonably suitable expression, flow, flavor, flair, freshness, and interest.

Sentence structure: The student has used somewhat appropriate sentence variety such as contrast, parallelism, balance, repetition, and exclamation.

Diction: The student usually uses specific and appropriate vocabulary, and is imaginative, vivid, and precise.

Language conventions: The student has for the most part correct spelling, grammar, punctuation, and avoids run-on sentences, etc.

Does not meet expectations

Content: The student only occasionally used accurate and pertinent content for the most part. The student was generally quite unconvincing, infrequently perceptive, and seldom showed imagination in expressing the content.

Development and organization: The student was not successful in constructing a coherent, unified, logical introduction, development and effective conclusion.

Paragraph development and organization: The student did not express a particularly clear statement of topic, nor was the student successful in constructing an effective development, nor varied paragraph structures sufficiently.

Point of view/ voice: The student's writing is usually inconsistent, rarely appropriate in mood and provides little to no emphasis to purpose and approach.

Style: The student's writing lacks suitable expression, flow, flavor, flair, freshness, and interest.

Sentence structure: The student has not used appropriate sentence variety such as contrast, parallelism, balance, repetition, and exclamation.

Diction: The student usually uses general rather than specific and appropriate vocabulary, and imagination, vividness, and preciseness is lacking.

Language conventions: The student has for the most part spelling, grammar, punctuation errors, and run-on sentences, etc., which impede meaning.

Unacceptable

Content: The student used inaccurate and irrelevant content for the most part. The student was unconvincing, not perceptive, and imagination in expressing the content was not evident.

Development and organization: The student was not successful in constructing a coherent, unified, logical introduction, or development or effective conclusion, or, unsuccessful in developing successfully all three.

Paragraph development and organization: The student did not express a clear statement of topic, nor was the student successful in constructing an effective development, nor varied paragraph structures.

Point of view/ voice: The student's writing is inconsistent, or inappropriate in mood or provides no emphasis to purpose and approach, or lacks all three.

Style: The student's writing has insufficient expression, flow, flavor, flair, freshness, and interest.

Sentence structure: The student has not used appropriate sentence variety such as contrast, parallelism, balance, repetition, and exclamation.

Diction: The student uses inappropriate vocabulary, and imagination, vividness, and preciseness is lacking entirely.

Language conventions: The student work is rife with spelling, grammar, punctuation errors, and run-on sentences.

It is good teaching practice to share the levels in the holistic scoring guides with the students first so that they have a common understanding for example of what "insufficient expression" means. Indeed, it is good practice to ensure that students understand any criteria or statements of outcomes or of standards that will be applied to their work (and peer- and self-assessment are particularly powerful ways of getting to grips with what such criteria really mean). Another good idea is to share copies of former students' work (with names whited out) to make it clearer what you want the students to aim for. If they can see the target, they will have a better chance of hitting it. Plagiarism (which is discussed alongside cheating in questions 11 & 12 in Chapter 9) can be avoided by a sensible policy on setting questions so that old questions are not reused. In this way old papers and essays become resources like any other learning resources, guides to students about good writing—and that's your point, isn't it? Chapter 9 has more to say on this topic.

Low Stakes and High Stakes: Summative, Formative, and Diagnostic Assessments

One kind of assessment is not preferable to or more appropriate than the other, each has different purposes and *the value of any assessment approach all depends on its purpose*. Each provides teachers and students with different kinds of information about student learning. In one case the information might be quite reliable but limited in scope; in another some rough and ready data are collected about what groups of students have got from the course; and in a third case, feedback on work-in-progress is given by the instructor and other students.

With that in mind we now turn to assessment methods or techniques. Some are obviously more appropriate when cheap, high reliability assessments are needed, and others blossom where reliability is not so important. While it is obviously best not to try to ask more of any technique than it can reasonably, efficiently and economically give, it is also desirable, as we will argue, to bring a range of methods to bear in the assessment of student learning in a course. That echoes a theme of the book that one way of fine tuning your teaching is to add more variety.

Tools for Making Fair Judgments

What are the different kinds of measures that can be used effectively? Let us now take a look at the variety of tools available and see why in fair student assessment practice, we need to use a multiple and variety of tools to make a fair judgment of what students know and can do. If we retain our focus on fair student assessment practice (better for them, better for learning, and better for you), then we will have less problem in living with our decisions on the assessment instruments we use.

4.11. Alternatives to MCTs

Open-book Exam

These kinds of exams do not focus on memorization and cramming. They allow the student to prepare thoughtfully for the exam ahead of time on questions that get at higher-order thinking skills such as analysis, critical thinking, evaluation, and synthesis. The bonus here is that it is stress reducing which allows learners to demonstrate what they know and can do without undue pressure. These exams allow more space for higher-level thinking to take place and reflection. Under a time limit in typical exams, it is very hard to reflect quickly (see also Chapter 2 on stress and learning).

The other important support for these kinds of exams is that they reflect the real world. When you need an answer to a questions, people go to the support they need, be a reference book, the Internet, or to some authority. The gist of it is that we know where to go to access it quickly. These exams promote student learning, but some students who work well under pressure, can make a good guess at what will be on the test (or pester the instructor to eke out information leading to it), and have good short-term memory, often prefer the traditional kind of exam of time limits and unseen questions.

There are two ways that you can conduct these exams. The first way the students are given the questions ahead of time and prepare their answers on their own time. On the exam day they rewrite their answers using their text for support and documentation.

The second way allows students to bring notes and textbooks into the exam to respond to never-before seen questions. The students still need to know the material well enough to access it under exam questions, yet they do not have to memorize every detail. Again, it is a stress reducer as well.

The Take-home Exam

This has the advantages of the open-book exam, but it is not written in class time, thereby allowing more instructional time for you and the students. Students can work at their own rate and comfort at home, and use relevant resources (texts, newspaper, www, experts, etc.). Some students prepare in pairs and groups, allowing for debate and discussion, although they have to submit papers and files that are individually written and they are told that software will be used to scan the papers for evidence of plagiarism. The competitive student, who works well under stress and time limits, will be at a relative disadvantage.

The instructor prepares the exam questions and distributes to the students. The students are usually given a week or two to write the exam. It is no advantage to give the students longer because students generally tend to leave it until the week or a few days before anyway. The students use resources from various sources. They then hand in a legible exam for you to read, considering it is not under a short time limit, and you might even be nicely surprised by an eyesight-saving word processed paper.

The Group Exam

As the name implies, this exam is written in small groups or pairs, usually at home in their own time. The kind of questions you give are not retrieval-based, but questions that seek higher levels of understanding such as synthesis and evaluation. The group discussion and argument that arise make for higher level thinking. The exam becomes another learning experience where students can use references and pooled resources that are unavailable during a traditional exam. This reduced stress exam is popular among students, always assuming that the group collaborates well. A suggested procedure is the following:

1. Assign groups ahead of time. A good way is to number off so that the randomness allows for knowledge, skill, and group dynamics.

2. Give the students the questions and the time in which the common paper must be handed in. Remind students to work to their strengths. In an ideal situation some students might be strong in understanding and articulating the question and efficient at lo cating information, another might be good at sifting through and analyzing it. Another good at synthesizing the main points, while another communicates well. However, sometimes some students work better doing this collaboratively instead of delegating tasks.

3. You might want to include peer-assessment to deter "easy riders;" see box 4.6 and check Box 6.3 on arriving at group marks from group assessment. Students need to know in advance how individual marks will be assigned.

When people think of assessment they usually equate it with the traditional kinds of tests such as selected-response, short answer, and essay tests, but kinds of tests are not limited to those, as Box 4.11 shows. Another kind, alternative or "authentic," performance assessment can be used as a complement to the traditional kind of tests to increase the richness of the assessment data to help you gain a more accurate idea of what students, given the chance to show their stuff, really know, understand, and can do.

These alternative assessment instruments are the power tools that can make life more rewarding and effective for you as a teacher. But why make life more complicated? Surely a multiple-choice test (MCT) should spit out a grade? Yes, it can be enough to provide a grade if you are willing to settle for an incomplete picture of the student's knowledge, understanding, and skills. While a multiple-choice test can be an effective tool, it cannot be used alone to provide an accurate picture of what a student knows and can do. For instance, students have "off days"; the questions might be posed in awkward ways and so even people who really knew the material "cold" find it hard to get in the flow, and others just lose their nerve and panic or freeze. Conversely there are lucky days when nothing can go wrong. The point is that to be confident about a level of performance we need to see that it can be repeated consistently a second or third time. Simply, we need multiple assessments rather than a one-shot event to make a reliable inference about any kind of achievement.

But what if the test-wise student can knock off MCTs as though they are second nature? Or if the student knows the stuff but is defeated by the MCT format? Selecting a response in a multiple-choice question is quite different from generating a response as one does in an essay question. By limiting the kind of tests to multiple choice only, for example, we advantage one student, but disadvantage another. Furthermore, MCTs simply cannot assess some of the complex learning outcomes that we rightly have in our courses and it takes enormous skill and effort to devise ones that get at "higher order" reasoning skills such as analysis, problem-working, critical thinking and evaluation, unless we reduce these complex activities to simple IQ-test puzzles, which bear little relation to the real-life activities. In the interests of validity—of assessing all of our program goals—we need a range of assessment tools because MCTs are best as tests of knowledge.

To illustrate, let us use the analogy of golf. One golfer might be consistently long and accurate off the tee, but loses it on the green. Another might be dynamite on the green, but pretty mediocre off the tee. If we make a judgment about someone who knows how to golf just by viewing the tee shots, one golfer is going to shine every time; similarly if we pin our judgment on putting skills, that's great news for that golfer who's deadly on the green. To get a valid inference about whether someone can golf or not, we need the complete picture—tee shots, fairway shots, and putts. Similarly for students, we need to know not only that they can select responses, but also that they can generate responses as well on a representative sample of the topics addressed in the course: and then that they can analyze, synthesize, criticize, work on problems and make judgements in the context of these topics. What this all boils down to is that we need a variety of tasks or performances testing a broad sample of areas of a course (golf or otherwise) to get a valid and reliable inference.

There is also the point that by providing a variety of assessment approaches, we recognize students' various learning styles: those who prefer objective tests (those with multiple-choice questions, true/false, matching, and fill-in-the-blank, can demonstrate in their preferred learning style what they know that why, while those who prefer a performance (such as an actual demonstration, essay, or project) can show you in that particular manner.

But surely that would mean setting a lot of slow-to-grade assignments, like essays? Yes. That is why we do not throw the baby out with the bath water; we need those MCTs as well to help assess the breadth of the content. Essays and projects do a better job of helping you assess other skills and the depth of understanding. Each has a strength, and by using various kinds of tools, we get the best of both worlds.

To sum: you need multiple assessments and a variety of assessment methods to judge students fairly and to get a valid inference of what they know, understand, and can do. Table 4.2 (p. 76) shows some of those methods. The first four are what might be called "objective" tests, although the idea of objectivity in assessment deserves more skeptical treatment than it normally receives—any test can be set in a harder or in an easier form, which makes us wonder what is then "objective" about the assessment—see also question 13 in Chapter 9. As an example of the subjectivity of testing, here is a question constructed by a pre-service teacher that was given to test Grade 4 students' social studies knowledge:

"Food in the Arctic is ..."
Children responded with "raw," "cold," "rare," "hard to find," "yucky." The "correct" response that the teacher expected was "expensive." Similarly, an

Table 4.2.
Strengths and Uses of a Selection of Common Assessment Tools

Test Type	Construction Strength	Marking Strength	Best Used For	Cautions
True/False	Quick and easy.	Quick and easy. Answer is either right or wrong.	Wide range of basic content knowledge, e.g., definitions.	50% chance of guessing the right answer! Unless time is short, prefer MCTs or short answer questions (in that order).
Multiple Choice	Very difficult and time-consuming to construct effective questions.	Quick and easy, particularly if machine scored sheets are used. Easy to analyze and bank, either by hand or by computer.	Wide range of basic content knowledge, recall, definitions Skilled testers can also use MCTs to get at "higher" skills such as analysis, problem working etc.	Exceptionally hard to write MCTs that do the intended job. For example, it's wearing to find at least four convincing alternatives for each question.
Matching	Related data is sometimes difficult to find, so can be difficult to match.	Quick and easy.	Fairly wide range of content knowledge. Knowledge and comprehension.	Best to have more possible matches than there are actual matches to improve reliability.
Fill in the blank	Quick and relatively easy.	Quick and easy.	Knowledge and comprehension.	The assumption is that there is one, right response that fills in the blank. Seldom is this the case. Can be an exercise in the student reading the teacher's mind.
Essay test, short-answer	Quick and easy to construct.	Time-consuming to mark. Easiest to mark if you have a clear scoring criteria.	Deeper understanding of content in real-world contexts. Exploring students' reasoning.	Can be very demanding on students unused to writing concisely and thoughtfully.
Performance-based, project, poster session, oral presentation, labs	Deeper understanding, problem-working, exploration of applications of ideas and techniques.	Gives access to areas not covered by MCTs but clear criteria for both instructor and student are essential.	Any assessments that try to get at what student achievement looks like in complex and real-world contexts.	Grading these assessments in a reliable way is expensive, slow and sometimes contentious.

experienced professor wrote this one for a third year university test:

"Lines on a tennis court are ...."

We think that the "correct" response for this one was "parallel."

Substantially longer lists of assessment methods and details of how to use them are to be found in *Assessing Learners in Higher Education* by Sally Brown and Peter Knight (1994), and *Assessment Essentials: Planning, Implementing, and Improving Assessment in Higher Education* by Catherine Palomba and Trudy Banta (1999).

How do you know which material best fits which kind of test? Let us look at some examples. If you teach a subject similar to descriptive statistics, you will be only too well aware that if something has a formula, it is instantly memorized and regurgitated by the students for the test. Their scores might really tell you very little about their grasp of descriptive statistics, since you do not know whether they will choose the right formula at the right time and be aware of the implications of, for example, giving a mean rather than the median or mode. You probably do want to know if they understand the application of descriptive statistics and then it's a good idea to use what is known as alternative or authentic assessments (anything other than objective test) and give them a performance test such as a project, case study analyses, oral or multimedia presentation, or a poster session, etc. It is also acceptable—even sensible—to use the traditional format of objective tests when they comprise meaningful multiple-choice questions that are located in a real-world context. These tests complement the evidence of the authentic performance assessments. Box 4.12 uses the Descriptive Statistics course to provide an example of a MCT that is embedded in a real-world context and that accesses students' understanding, not just their recall of inert information. It will be seen that the aim is to use a range of methods to get at comprehension and application, as well as at the inevitable, overworked "knowledge" category. In other cases different methods might have been used to get at, say,

- Analysis (analyzing a chart).
- Synthesis (putting the information together).
- Evaluation (making an inference or judgement from the information).
- Comprehension (this is understanding of why something happened when).
- Application questions (these allow students to apply the recalled and comprehended material to a practical situation or context, for example a car costs $2000. How much will 10 monthly payments be?)
- Knowledge, (this is recognition or recall such as dates, places—greatly overassessed on a global scale).

4.12. A MCT Designed to Assess Understanding of Descriptive Statistics

It was almost report card and parent-teacher interview time at Windy City High School. Several teachers were in the midst of marking and calculating student results of their students' final tests. The principal, Ms. Austin who had taken Evaluation 3604 from The University of Lethbridge a short time ago, was adamant that the teachers report accurate statistical results to her and the parents and students. Ms. Austin met individually with her teachers on staff to check these results

1. When Ms. Austin studied Ms. Doucet's scores she noticed that Ms. Doucet's set of scores was perfectly symmetrical around a middle point. Therefore she was certain that the
    a) mean, median and mode were all equal
    b) mean = median
    c) median = mode
    d) mode = mean.

In preparation for report cards Mr. Colbeck gave a unit test to his Grade 7 math class of 25 students. His statistics on this test read as follows:
    Mean =14.4
    Median =15
    Mode =15
    Range =15
    Variance =14.67
    Standard Deviation =3.83

Use the data in the table to answer questions 2, 3, and 4.

2. Mr. Colbeck was able to report with reasonable certainty that:
    a. The resulting histogram representation was not bimodal.
    b. All of the students received a score of at least 10.
    c. Approximately two-thirds of his class failed.
    d. The top score in the class was 15.

3. Ms. Austin correctly notes that:
    a. Nobody failed the test!
    b. Nobody scored higher than 19.
    c. All of your students scored between 6 and 20.
    d. Your class scored on a near-perfect symmetrical curve.

4. Mr. Colbeck looks at his analysis and decides that:

    a. Having an identical median and mode was an indication that his test was geared towards the majority of the class.
    b. More students scored higher than the class average than those who scored less.
    c. All of his students should have passed this test.
    d. His test was too difficult.

(For more guidance on writing MCTs see Stiggins' 1997 *Student-Centered Classroom Assessment*).

Although assessments might often be quickly written, they are the best and fairest reflection of your course goals and learning outcomes if they are systematically constructed. Box 4.13 (p. 80) is the blueprint, or plan, or specification for an end-of-course examination. As with the overall assessment plan for the course it is as well to share this with students so that they can see exactly what is being valued — so that they can see what the *real* curriculum is—and direct their learning accordingly. Some people will say that this encourages learning to the test. Precisely. Where the test or assessment plan is a good, valid and well-conceived representation of your goals and learning outcomes, then teaching and learning to the test are desirable, not something to be defensive about. A Psychology department in a top ranked British university used to begin the year by posting the (long and complex) examination paper on the notice board. The reasoning was that if students learned enough to answer it, then they should pass the course: nasty surprises were seen as the product of some non-psychological thinking about the assessment of human learning and probably indicative of some personality faults on the part of those who favored an assessment-as-ambush approach.

Sometimes your colleagues might find this threatening because students will ask them for their test blueprint. It causes them some problems. One is that they have not developed one; second is that they believe that somehow you are giving away the tests. What you are really doing is indicating that you are not testing haphazardly, that you are organized, and that you're earnest in helping the students do as well as they can. Yes, you are actually "on their side" and being fair about your testing practice. You gain an enormous amount of respect by doing this fairly simple step.

From the Assessment of Learning to Numbers and Letters

However much you want to use assessments to improve students' learning and to give priority to low stakes, formative and diagnostic assessments, we are all in a system that wants high stakes summative procedures that deliver numbers or letters which are then used—often quite inappropriately—as indicators of the efficiency and effectiveness of different parts of the higher education system. This is not the place to argue that assessment data of the sort that are routinely generated are very poor performance indicators and way removed from signals of quality education. In this concluding section we simply look at the mechanics of reliable marking (a necessity in high stakes assessment) and of putting grades to marks.

In practice, "objective" tests of information, especially MCTs, can be marked with total reliability. They tend not to be very good as indicators of what students have learned, unless, of course, they have learned little more than information. In some areas that is not a cause for concern, although it is increasingly discussed in Britain, New Zealand, and Australia, where there is discussion of how assessments can be valid judgments of progress towards complex curriculum goals. And here is the problem: the more complex the goals and the more that inference is needed

4.13. An Examination Blueprint

Focus				Assessment Method				
K	C	A	Content Area	Multiple Choice	Matching	True-False	Short Answer	Total
	12*		Taxonomy	12*				1
	26		Blueprinting-unit/test	26				1
	14, 16, 28, 29		Validity & reliability	14, 16, 28, 29				4
	25		Essay-type questions: pros, cons, and construction	25				1
	11		Holistic/analytic scoring	11				1
1, 20, 21, 22, 23, 24	10, 15		Objective questions: advantages & disadvantages	10, 15	20, 21, 22, 23, 24	1		8
	13, 30	32	Question construction	13, 30			32	3
	17	3, 4, 4, 6, 7, 8, 9	Item analysis	3, 4, 5, 6, 7, 8, 9, 17				8
	18, 19, 27	33	Descriptive statistics	18, 19, 27			33	4
2		31	Test construction			2	31	2
7	16	10		23	5	2	3	33

Notes: K = Knowledge; C = Comprehension; A = Application; * = question numbers

to judge attainment, the harder and costlier it is to have high levels of reliability.

Reliability can be enhanced —but never guaranteed to the same levels as MCT marking—by all or some of the devices shown in Box 4.14, *each of which is costly in some way or another.* In many British universities all exam essays have to be independently marked by at least two faculty members and the same rule should arguably apply to all high stakes assignments, unless they are "objective answer" tests.

4.14. *Reliable Grading of Complex Assessments (Principally Essays)*

Here are some marking tips that you might find useful.

1. When marking tests consisting of several complex questions (not MCTs), there is a lot to be said for marking all the same questions at once—mark all questions one before going on to questions 2 (or which ever order you want to do this). It is easier and more reliable to have one scoring guide in your mind as you mark—and quicker, too.
2. It is a good idea to have students use only their ID number. You can match it to the class list after you've marked the papers and confirmed that the marks given are fair.
3. After you have marked a few questions, check that you are sticking to your scoring guide. This is the time to fine tune your scoring guide.
4. Once you have get into the rhythm (the first few papers take longer to mark than the others because you're not familiar with the rubric yet) *set yourself a reasonable time for each question and make yourself stick to it.* You might start out taking 15 minutes per essay question (too long!), but once you are comfortable, set your mean time per question to no more than 10 minutes. It is a good motivator and prevents you from wasting time. The occasional disorganized or illegible paper might take longer, others will take less time.
5. When you have completed your marking, review a sample (no more than 10% should do it) to check your reliability. Some instructors mark easier as they go; others mark harder. Some are fooled by neat handwriting or length of paper. If neat handwriting or presentation is not one of the criterion, then do not include it in your marking. Having a colleague to do this is even better to check reliability. Do not be surprised that if you have a solid rubric that you will be within a few marks from each other for the papers. However, don't expect to have exactly the same mark — human judgement can get you in the same ball park but is less likely to get you on the same blades of grass.
6. Record your marks on your spreadsheet. If students will take notice of feedback from this assessment, consider giving the class five or six headline points for improvement to and perhaps offering each student one or two personal pointers for development. In any case, it is a good idea to make yourself a note of how to improve your teaching next time around and about how the assessment might be revised for future use.
7. Distribute papers in class yourself or arrange a supervised pickup point to keep the students' marks confidential.

Another way of increasing the reliability of a grade is to ensure that it is based upon plenty of assessments, including repeated assessments of the same learning outcome. Not only is this time-consuming for everyone, it can be practically impossible when courses are only a semester long. In other words, once we move away from the assessment of information, reliability and certainly fall off sharply, unless considerable effort is expended on developing and using criteria, using multiple markers and having repeated assessments of the same learning outcome. That should help to debunk the idea that assessments and the grades that are based on them are anything more than informed guesses about achievement. It also explains why assessment is best seen as a way of giving people suggestions for further learning than it is as a way of affirming what they really understand and can do. Grades are best guesses. Some best guesses are a lot better than most.

Where final course grades are the result of distributing raw scores into categories according to some notion of what proportion of A's there *ought* to be if standards are to be preserved, then the grades are pretty untrustworthy guesses, as Box 4.15 suggests.

4.15. Grading on the Curve?

As at the last judgment, students are sorted into the wheat and the chaff. Rewards of A's and B's go out to the good, and punishments of F's are doled out to the bad. "Gifts" of D's (D's are always gifts) are metered out, and C's (that wonderfully tepid grade) are bestowed on those whose names teachers can barely remember. (Majesky, 1993, p. 88)

A grade can be an aggregate score for a course, or it can be for a discrete paper project, presentation, etc. Different rules for combining different scores in different combinations, and then the rules for turning those figures into grades all have a considerable and seldom-acknowledged effect on the final grade. But, however it is done, grading should never be used as punishment or a weapon to shape the students up. This has no educational value. Find another way to punish the student if you must. If it is used to prompt greater effort, research shows that instead, the student withdraws to save face, or gives up.

Grading should always be done in reference to learning criteria, never "on the curve" Guskey (1996). In other words, criterion-referenced grading is better than norm-referenced grading (which is when a grade only says where a student's scores lie in the class rank order). The idea that grades should fit the normal distribution pattern (often called "the bell curve" because of the shape of its graph) has nothing to do with assessing students' knowledge and understanding; the bell curve just provides information the relative standing of students within a group. *Grades distributed according to this curve almost certainly don't mean what you think and probably do mean things you hadn't realized.* However, norm referencing, or grading on the curve, has gotten mixed up with some faulty ideas about standards and is now quite common. When faculty meetings heat up over this issue, it can be useful to recall that a norm-referenced grade is an artifact that bears no clear relation to valid standards and is psychometrically indefensible at the classroom level (Wiggins, 1993).

In terms of the effect upon learning, grading on the curve often causes so much competitiveness that any attempt to promote collaborative learning is thwarted. Students quickly see that helping others and sharing information is detrimental to their grade (the name of the bell curve game is "beggar my neighbor"), so any good intentions of promoting collaboration fail miserably.

A final irony. Although the normal distribution of some phenomena may be graphed as a bell curve, statisticians are beginning to conclude that the "normal" distribution of many social data sets *does not* have that shape. Their "normal" distribution is quite different from the one in the classical statistics based on "normal" science.

---

5. Presentations

Preview

We are much happier to talk about presentations than lectures. The former are varied and engaging, whereas lectures seem like faintly embarrassing leftovers from another age.

Presentations are one way of conveying information but other ways can be more congenial and more efficient, according to students' preferred learning behaviors, motivations, intelligences and approaches to learning.

Presentations are best as ways of providing frameworks for understanding; for ensuring that learning has a social and interactive side; and as rituals that help to organize and pace student learning.

Rightly or wrongly, the higher education community takes the ability to do good presentations as a sensitive indicator of your teaching quality. Our headline points about doing good presentations is:

- Concentrate on giving the big picture.
- Plan for variety of approach within a presentation.
- Your body language and voice say more than any words you will use, so take a sharp look at how you breathe, hold yourself and speak.
- Introductions should be like this preview—they should lay out the headline points.
- Keywords are variety, clarity, interactivity, and enthusiasm.
- Check out what students are learning using methods described in Chapter 4 and make it possible for students to contact you, preferably electronically, between presentations.

The Death of the Lecture

What we call "presentations," people would usually call lectures. We prefer to talk of presentations because it does not carry the baggage of the word "lectures." The word "lecture" comes from the Latin word for reading, and if there is one thing a presentation should not be, it is a reading. Nor should it be an unbroken patter by the lecturer, relying on the speech alone, and requiring the students to do little more than transcribe the spoken into the written word.

Before setting out a view of the characteristics of a good presentation, we want to criticize an often-voiced view that lectures are inefficient and ineffective.

To do that, we want to use a very simple model of learning. Learning, we suggest, involves getting information and working on it. As we said in Chapter 2, the ways in which we get and work upon information are affected by the motivation to learn, by our learning approaches, by the circumstances in which learning takes place (the student learning environment), by our previous understandings, and by our experience as learners and the practices it has given us. In this chapter we concentrate on the part lectures can have in helping students to get information and then to work upon it in order to understand and apply it.

Getting Information

Information can be got from a number of sources. Traditionally these have been print and lectures. A criticism of lectures has been that fast readers can get the information more swiftly through a book or articles. Agreed, although many print sources actually assume high levels of prior understanding. Lectures might be inefficient ways of trying to do what print does. Other media also compete with lectures to carry information. Video has an immediacy that appeals and it is helpful to people who are more sensitive to visual sources. The web gives access to troves of information, which is typically print-on-the screen, although multimedia is fast changing that.

The lecture is the least flexible of these methods of getting information, since it depends on the audience assembling at the same time and in the same place as the lecturer. While it is true that satellite transmission and other methods of broadcasting mean that the audience can be enlarged and while recording allows people to play the lecture at their convenience, these ways of making the lecture more flexible have a disadvantage. They lose the real-time quality of a lecture, the sense of an event, the interaction between the lecturer and the audience, and the gathering of people with a shared purpose. Behind this objection is the idea that learning is not a solitary activity: or rather, it *is* possible to learn seated at a computer, but for most people the human quality that comes from the presence of others and interaction with them is important. For that reason, we suggest that students should be expected to get information from a variety of sources *and* that presentations should be one of those on offer. Since people learn in different ways, we are reluctant to insist that everybody should have to attend a lecture, just as we would not want to make everyone use the web (unless that in itself were a course goal), or watch videos. And, we ought not to lose sight of the fact that lectures involve real people in real time and, because they are events, they provide something of a rhythm for learning. We suggest that if the social and ritual functions of presentations are lost, then the experience of learning is changed and, we think, changed for the worse.

Presentations as Advance Organizers for Working on Information

Yet, there are still problems with this attempt to rehabilitate presentations.

For example, there are real problems with saying that they are the best--or even a very effective—way of conveying large amounts of factual information that students will then both understand and retain. However, we do say that lectures and presentations are excellent as ways of providing students with:

- A conceptual framework for a topic
- An indication of how key areas of information fit into that framework
- An indication of the strengths and problems with the framework
- A preview of implications of a framework
- A model of the ways in which people in a discipline develop understandings, test and apply them

The suggestion is that lectures have been criticized for not doing well things that they ought not to be trying to do. We see them as "advance organizers," sketches of a territory that orient students to the task of working on information that they are going to be acquiring. If they are seen like that, then good presentations will:

- provide frameworks, not details; indicate points where analysis, criticism and evaluation would be fruitful, but do not try to complete those activities.
- are one part of a planned set of learning activities.
- involve the audience in thinking, rather than requiring them to be no more than stenographers.
- are not readings, but events that use a range of activities and media to help people to learn well (and different people have different learning styles, as we saw in Chapter 3, which means that they are sensitive to different ways of conveying information).
- are social occasions, with interaction between presenter and audience and between members of the audience.
- have established roles in setting the pace of learning and in structuring it
- should be optional. What matters is that learners get the frameworks. How they get the frameworks is for them to decide.

An excellent source of further advice on the nuts-and-bolts business of making presentations is Michael Gelb's *Present Yourself* (1988).

Planning Presentations

We all have experience of writing the abstract of a journal article, explaining what the article argues and indicating the main stages of the argument. Planning a presentation is like writing an abstract—it is about identifying the key points.

If you have problems identifying identify key points, it is likely that you are thinking in terms of an information-conveying lecture. There are alternative ways of conveying that information and it might be a good idea to use them, rather than to try to convey it orally.

We suggest that answering the following questions is a good basis from which to start planning a presentation:

- What concepts or ideas do people need to understand in order to make sense of this topic? (or, in some subjects, "what skills, procedures or qualities do people need to develop in order to be able to do this?")
- How does this connect with what they already understand or are already able to do? (Chapter 4 made suggestions for checking out the level of understanding students bring with them).
- Why is this topic/skill/procedure/quality important: what is its significance?
- What information, or stories, or visual, or audio material illustrate these concepts, procedures, or skills?
- What are the main strengths and weaknesses of these concepts, or the main uses and limits of these skills?
- Can connections be made between this material and issues of significance, especially with "real world" and live issues?

In other words, we are saying that purposeful presentations begin with thinking big, with identifying the main, or structural, features of a topic, skill or procedure. The presentation should be planned to address these structural features, the expectation being that the students will themselves add information to this framework and then work upon it as they do tasks you have designed to have them analyze, criticize, evaluate, and apply it.

Planning will also involve thinking about ways of sharing this framework, about what you could call "teaching methods." It is important to think about ways of presenting ideas that do not rely on words alone, as well as to think about the pace and sequence of activities. For example, try to think of diagrams, sketches, video clips or slides that could illustrate points and connections. Some people learn best by doing. This can be hard to build into presentations, but it is still worth looking for small activities for students to do that consolidate ideas in the presentation. Box 5.1 contains an example of "doing" techniques used in a social science presentation.

Look also at the pattern of the presentation. There is a great deal of research that shows that after 15-20 minutes listening to someone talk, our attention fades. Is it possible to organize the presentation into segments of 15-20 minutes (there is no advantage in breaking it into smaller segments), by using breathing spaces, review activities, thinking tasks, Classroom Assessment Techniques (Chapter 4), discussion tasks (Chapter 6) or small writing activities?

A word of warning. Many students have got well formed expectations of a presentation. They expect a presentation to be a lecture that gives them all the information they need, making further reading a luxury. In other words, they approach presentations in the spirit of surface learning. If you follow the approach to presentations that we are advocating, it is vital that students know, from the start:

- What you are trying to do in presentations.
- What you are not trying to do in presentations.
- What you expect them to do by way of further study and work in seminars and laboratories, and how these activities connect with the presentations.
- Why you take this approach.

This message will need to be repeated more than once in a course and should certainly be in the course syllabus or handbook. Ideally, it should pervade a complete program.

Before the Presentation

Presentations rely on your presence and voice. Frequently, we plan what we are going to say and do nothing to tune the way we say it. That is unfortunate,

---

since there is some research that suggests that students make judgments about our teaching effectiveness on the basis of our body language, rather than on the content of what we say. What is more, the judgments they make within the first seconds of our first presentation correlate remarkably strongly with the judgments they make in the end-of-course evaluations. Frequently, students say that a good instructor is "interested," "enthusiastic," "approachable," "friendly," and "has a sense of humor." Each of these qualities is conveyed by our body language, the ways in which we hold and present ourselves. The person who adopts defensive body language, sheltering behind the podium (and who needs a podium?), with a low, monotonous voice, little movement or energy, stiff face, hunched posture; who avoids eye contact and smiles seldom, will have a hard time seeming friendly, approachable, enthusiastic, or interested. And even the best jokes fall flat where timing, posture and expression are out. This section is about self-presentation and the use of voice. Both matter. We are not saying that successful presentations depend on being like a TV evangelist or a snake-oil merchant. Charisma is an optional extra. We are saying that successful presentations depend on not *looking* scared or bored, and on speaking with clarity and variety. Four suggestions are:

- Defensive, tense, and unconfident body language sends out all sorts of signals that invite a poor reaction from students. Consider, for example, the ways in which you use your hands and arms, and whether you use movements that draw learners in to the presentation. What about your stance: is it upright, without being stiff? Does it allow you to make eye contact with the audience? Can you breathe easily from your abdomen, rather than from your upper chest? If it helps you to feel confident *and* relaxed, dress up for a class – some men will even wear a suit and bow tie for the occasion. You might find it useful to look at a book on T'ai Chi, the Alexander Technique, or Yoga to see what a good body posture looks like.

- Half an hour before the class, take ten minutes to deliberately relax—breathing exercises, sitting still, listening to calming music, and going for a walk can all help. During that time, think through the coming session, looking for tricky junctures and wondering about good hooks and lines to use. But the aim is to do this calmly, not with agitation. Nor is it intended to be a route to sleepiness and passivity. It is more in the nature of a focusing exercise.

- You might wish to have some music playing gently as students assemble. The work of composers such as Bach, Mozart, and Corelli is often recommended. This sets a good mood, both for you and them.

- If you have never done microteaching, where your teaching is video recorded for you to watch, it is advisable to do it now, so as to see how your body works when you are teaching. We suggest you review the video with the sound turned off. Then with the sound off, fast forward the tape, which should make your mannerisms and quirks stand out. If you can bear to watch the tape with a friend who can talk with you about the way you present yourself, so much the better.

Breathing well is the key to speaking well. To check your breathing style, stand as if you were about to speak to an audience and rest the palm of one hand on your chest and the other on your abdomen, slightly above your navel. Breathe and notice how your hands move. Good speaking is easiest when you find that it is the hand on your abdomen that moves when you inhale, not the hand on your chest. Abdominal breathing is important for voice pitch, volume, and duration: clavicular breaths tend to be shallower, which means that you can say less per breath, that you will speak with a shriller voice and that you will have to strain more in order to produce a louder voice.

Relaxed posture, especially relaxation in the abdomen, neck and jaw, is important for good voice production. A motto is "breathe with a soft belly."

Practice to vary the volume, pace and pitch of your voice. Experienced school teachers will often speak more softly when they want attention. Lowering the volume can be used to emphasize points as well as to command attention. Likewise with pace. Pause between sentences for dramatic effect and emphasis. If lists are given for illustrative purposes, speed up. Change the intonation. Sometimes enthusiastic, sometimes emphatic, sometimes querulous, and sometimes humorous. All of these vocal variations add to the quality of a presentation and, for most of us, all demand practice.

A variant of microteaching is to have part of a presentation recorded on audiotape from the back of the room and then to listen to yourself. Concentrate on the way you are speaking, not on the content. How could the delivery be improved?—think volume, pace, and pitch. Further guidelines on good presentational style are in Box 7.2 and Chapter 9, question 14 addresses some teachers' fears that in taking on this sort of presentational role they might be losing something of themselves.

Setting a Scene

We suggest that before you start a presentation, you aim to:

- Check that audiovisual equipment works, is focused and can be heard and seen from the back of the room.

- If possible, be in the room ten minutes before the start of the class to mingle with the students and chat. This is a vital piece of public relations work with large classes and makes good sense with smaller ones too.

- Have something on the board or screen for students who are not talking with you to think about or do as they come in to the class.

- Start on time—set this habit from the beginning of your class.

Leave routine announcements and class business until later. Begin, if you have the skill, with an attention catching maxim, story, point of view, cartoon, video clip, or the like. The way that Stephen Jay Gould introduces his scholarly and controversial science essays is for Peter a model of good writing that he also calls to mind when he is trying to find ways of beginning and ending his presentations. Then (or as your beginning if you cannot think of a better way of starting) make links to what was covered in the earlier sessions and preview what is to come. Here it is not very helpful to say that we are going to look at this and then that and finish with something else. It is far better to summarize the argument and endpoint of the presentation. Many of the best presenters will put the structure of the presentation on an OHT and showing that at the beginning of the session, and returning to it at key points in the presentation to help people see how the parts fit to the whole.

The guiding principle is "tell them what you're going to tell them, tell them, and tell them you've told them."

The Body of the Lecture

A lot of what we say here could equally well have gone into the "Planning" section. Novice teachers and those trying to change their style do need to look at these matters at the planning stage. Those who are expert in this style of presentation seem to "just do it." Lucky them!

We begin with a reminder to intersperse your presentation with active learning techniques. Examples of these include: Classroom Assessment Techniques; questions for the students to talk about with their neighbors; two-minute "stand up, stretch and breathe" sessions; time for students to review their notes (or perhaps to review each other's notes); "buzz group" activities; and questions for students to consider or to talk about with their neighbors. Use a variety of media: talk, slides and OHTs, handouts, computer programs (in anatomy, for example), mini-presentations from students, and video clips. All of these help to break up the monotony that accompanies even the best presenter who talks too long.

Students like presenters who explain things clearly. So:

- Do not rush or try to cover too much information.
- Concentrate on making sense of the "big picture."
- Do repeat yourself, preferably varying the words.
- Use examples, similes, and metaphors.
- Make connections with "real life," if possible.

There are also some points of technique to keep in mind in the body of the presentation:

Overhead Projector Transparencies

- Use them if they will enhance your presentation.
- Unless the projection quality is so loathsome that you should not be using OHTs, assume students can read. You do not have to sound out all the words on your transparency.
- Keep the number of OHTs small rather than large, and try to limit the number of points on each transparency—a rule of six slides, each with no more than six points, has been suggested.

Involving the Audience — Questions

It is possible, even with 800 students, to ask and to invite questions. Some professors plant questions in the audience so as to ease things along.

When asking, wait for answers, look around the audience, repeat the question, ask the questioner's name and thank him or her. When receiving questions, again repeat them for all to hear and thank the questioner. (Some professors who teach "small" large classes try to learn students' names, often by having a board on which photographs of all the students are displayed; others take their photos [with student permission granted] using a digital camera and downloading the photos onto their computer for easy reference.).

There are risks when you invite students to raise questions. The danger is not that they might ask something you cannot answer because there are at least four good responses there. One is to say that you do not know but will find out and report back. A second is to ask if anyone else in the room can answer. A third is to require the students to find answers before the next session. Fourth, invite the student to approach you at the end of the presentation, explaining that the answer involves an explanation that goes beyond your goals for this presentation but which you are delighted to share with the questioner and anyone else who wishes to listen. The biggest dangers are being thrown off course and losing control of the presentation's timing. Have some sense of what you might do if you sickeningly realize that questioning has thrown you seriously off-course. What can be cut entirely or moved into the next session or allocated to an assignment? It is always a good idea to have some sense of what you might do if you find yourself with 15 minutes to go and half of what you planned still to cover.

Handouts and Support Materials

The principle of trying to say less and to say it better means that more use has to be made of supplemental materials such as handouts. They can list key points and connections; contain an outline of the lecture; draw attention to terms to be learned and to recommended reading.

Some people have surprising logistical problems getting these materials to students. The best advice is to establish a system in the first session and expect people to use it thereafter. Common methods are to expect students to pick papers up from tables on entry (make sure you have at least two lines running or there will be awful congestion); to have student helpers give paper out to those coming in to the presentation; to put copies of handouts on the end seat of each aisle and expect people to pick up copies as they make their way to their seat; and where this makes good teaching sense, to have people collect handouts on exit (this should be used for supplementary, follow-up and extension material only).

Classroom Incivilities

This phrase comes from Robert Boice's excellent 1996 book *Title!!* It refers to student behaviors that can disturb, disrupt or destroy a presentation—talking, nudging others, lounging around in a bored, even hostile manner, and taking or making phone calls. We find these behaviors offensive, although you might not agree, in which case the rest of this section can be skipped.

Educators are familiar with these classroom incivilities in high schools and often say that they are mainly caused by poor curriculum and poor instruction. This is often true but it is not necessarily true. Another common explanation is that the teacher has failed to set out rules and expectations, has failed to explain why they are fair expectations, has done so in a confrontational manner, or has failed to act on breaches of those expectations. We see the same applying to higher education classes and suggest the following strategies.

- At the beginning of the course you will be explaining your approach to presentations (see above). This is a good point to say that the intention is to cover topics in a way that students will not find elsewhere. Therefore, it is in the group's interest that only one person speaks at a time. Another way to deal with this is to expect students to speak one at a time. The first time they don't, make the point that a smooth and well run discussion relies very much on people taking turns at speaking.
- If this expectation is violated there are a number of public strategies that can be used. Use these where you do not expect a confrontation that you cannot win (and schoolteachers create disciplinary problems by trying to deal, in front of the whole class, with things that need to be dealt with in a lower-key way in private). They include: Make eye contact with the person who is talking and nod, or signal for quiet with your hand; stop talking, look and

wait for silence; repeat your expectation and the reason behind it; ask the person to be quiet or desist.

- If public strategies do not work—and even if they do—private strategies can be effective. They involve talking *on a one-to-one basis* with uncivil students. The talk should not force the student into a corner. Explain how the behavior affects your ability to present well and other students' concentration.
- Remove uncivil students from the class. Schoolteachers can rarely get rid of troublesome students. University teachers have greater powers, if they chose to use them. Some see this as a sign of weakness. The alternative view, which we hold, is that it is far weaker to put up with unacceptable behavior.

And in the End

At least, summarize, in words, what you have said. Better still, summarize it and connect it to the "big picture"—How do these functions contribute to the working of the whole? What do they tell us, if anything, about the nature of the discipline? How do they impact on theories? What implications might be raised by these points? If possible, use a figure or chart: better still, have a partly completed chart or figure as a handout, with the presentation finishing with students completing it.

Alternatively, use the Classroom Assessment Technique of "the minute paper" in which students have a time to review their notes and then a minute to write down a summary of the session. You could collect all papers, which you will return later, and read a sample of them if the class is a large one. Then use what you find to shape the beginning of your next presentation.

In all cases, summarizing also involves reaffirming the links between what has happened in the presentation and the individual study that is to be done and seminar or laboratory work.

And After

Some professors build good relationships with students by making it clear that their doors are open to inquiries; by putting their Internet addresses in the course handbook and inviting students to mail electronic queries to them; and by giving out their home phone number for students to use if need be (and there seem to be few reports of this being abused).

It is also a good idea to do some form of course evaluation earlier than is usual—say in week 2 or 3 and again some five weeks later—because if you are off beam in presentations the error has high visibility and greater consequences than it does if you miss the mark in tutorials or other small group settings. In large classes, a sample of fifty evaluation sheets will be sufficient to highlight things that

5.2. Presentation effectiveness rating scale.

Your answers will be used to help make future presentations better for you. You should not put your name on this sheet.

	Yes	No
A1. Did the presenter do anything to improve the quality of the environment in which the presentation took place? (For example, rearranging furniture, playing music, having an attractive slide on when you entered the room.)		
A2. Was the presenter in the room early (if it was possible to get into the room early)?		
A3. Did the session finish in good time and without undue haste towards the end?		
A4. Was the presentation linked to the readings and to any small group sessions such as tutorials?		
Mean score for section A (Yes = 1, No = 0)		
B1. Did the presenter look interested and at ease?		
B2. Did the presenter convey enthusiasm, for example by body language and tone of voice?		
B3. Did the presenter make eye contact with people in the audience?		
B4. Was the presenter audible?		
B5. Was the presenter's voice interesting and varied in tone, pace, and pitch?		
B6. Did the presenter read out the presentation?		
Mean score for section B (Yes = 1, No = 0)		
C1. Did the presentation begin with a preview of the position that would be developed in this session?		
C2. Were legible visual materials used?		
C3. Were there breaks in the presentation that involved you in thinking, doing something, or in discussing a question with others in the audience?		
C4. Was the presentation easy to follow?		
C5. Are your notes mainly filled with ideas about concepts, their applications, problems, connections, and implications?		
C6. Did the presenter ask you, the students, questions?		
Mean score for section C (Yes = 1, No = 0)		
Please write up to three things that could be done to improve presentations for next year's class. 1. 2 3.		

need attention, as well as to remind you of things that are going well. The form in Box 5.2 is intended to direct your attention to areas for improvement, not to produce a pretty-unhelpful numerical score. We suggest that the key things to look at are the mean scores for each of the three sections and the tally of the write-in suggestions about improvement (and one of us is able to have course evaluations that *only* involve students making suggestions for how the course could be better next time around). Under no circumstances should the scores on this sheet—or on any other evaluation sheet—be used to make simple comparisons between different teachers: comparisons are attractive, easy to do and usually misleading and therefore unfair.

Two Retractions and an Extension

There are two situations where we need to retract some of the advice we have given. The first is where you are constrained to give presentations that do little more than convey information, and the other is where there are no seminars or small group sessions to complement the presentations.

It is quite common in some subjects for freshman courses to be dominated by the aim of conveying information. Even where the course aims speak of more ambitious things, the assessment plan often plainly shows that it is information, and only information, that is valued. That is at variance with the approach to presentations that we have been recommending. Although it would be good if this practice changed, realistically, we acknowledge that it is well embedded in departmental cultures.

Nevertheless, we suggest that there are principles in what we have recommended that can be applied to presentations that are information-led. The points about not trying to cover too much (which would involve focusing on the most difficult points, leaving students to get other information from texts); about presenting in a variety of ways; about providing breaks and a variety of activities; about examining the use of voice and body language; and about getting feedback from students, are particularly salient.

Those points apply just as much where there are no tutorials or other small group activities to complement the presentation. In this case, though, there is a particular problem in getting students to work with the information, which we have portrayed as the goal of smaller group sessions. Here we repeat a point from Chapter 4, namely that the quality of the assessment procedures is important. Good, thoughtful tasks can get students, individually or in small groups, to work through the framework laid out in the presentation. There is fuller consideration of bringing interactivity into your teaching in the next chapter.

Lastly, we briefly extend the ideas of this chapter to cover web presentations. These are growing in popularity, sophistication, and ease of construction. While

---

our suggestions about voice and body have little direct applicability to web presentations, the other points about clarity of purpose, variety, using the presentation to handle frameworks that are not well covered in information books, and being responsive to student feedback, all hold true for web presentations.

While we will not go into a detailed analysis of the relative merits of web and face-to-face presentations, we will end this chapter with the claim that if face-to-face presentations are not good performances, then they will be displaced by web presentations. Web presentations have enormous advantages in terms of convenience. If the face-to-face presentation is to survive in competition with virtual universities and web presentations, then they need to be appreciated, by the students, as good occasions. Weak presentations and the classic lecture are very vulnerable to multimedia web presentations, as are traditional universities themselves. There is, then, a very strong sense in which universities have a considerable interest in ensuring better presentations, unless, of course, they are themselves committed to the web route.

6. Maximizing Student Interaction: Group Work and Other Interactive Learning Techniques

Preview

Box 6.1 (p. 100) gives seven reasons why good teachers plan for interactive work in the classroom.

. There are descriptions of nine simple interactive learning techniques that can be used into presentations and six types of group learning projects are outlined.

Boxes 6.3 (p. 112) and 6.4 (p. 113) introduce the topic of assigning marks to group learning activities.

Introduction

Some form of group work or student-student interaction can be managed even in quite large enrollment classes (up to approximately 200 students), and can actually enhance computer-based, selected-response evaluation that is so often an inevitable feature of large classrooms. But why bother?

Imagine you are an employer of university graduates of all kinds. You know your business and you are prepared to take responsibility for on-the-job training. What kind of student would you want to hire? When employers the USA, UK, Australia, Canada, or New Zealand are asked what qualities make a student employable, they usually emphasize a range of non-cognitive qualities, and invariably put especial emphasis on interpersonal skills, getting along with others and working within a team. And that theme is also worked through bestselling business and self-fulfillment books, such as those by Daniel Goleman, Tom Peters, and Peter Senge. In addition, there are many texts, manuals and papers on teaching and learning that encourage and advocate cooperative learning through group activities.

Employability is only part of it. Learning to work with others is known, not just to help students become "intelligent," but according to Johnson, Johnson, and Holubec (1994), group work will raise the achievement level of all students, including both the gifted and the challenged; it will help develop the social skills of students as they develop positive relationships with others; and it will help students develop the psychological maturity and cognitive skills required for high level performance in all areas of life. We have asked students questions about working within groups in university courses since 1995 and have cabinet loads of positive responses, including:

"The class was enormous but well organized into groups which brought it down to a smaller learning community and I felt I did better than I would have working alone."

"Group work was good for meeting people and learning to work together."

"We learned more without really realizing we had because it was fun."

Yet it is nothing less than amazing that the majority of courses taught in universities in the English-speaking world still largely follow a traditional lecture format, where students behave as passive receptors except when competing on tests and assignments. In some places there is a whiff of disapproval about students learning from or with each other on the grounds that plagiarism, idleness and fun might then seep in.

This chapter shows that there are many ways of helping students to learn with and from each other. As faculty we learn interactively, just as the three of us have each learned by the shared experience of thinking and writing this book. So too students can learn more efficiently and better when they work with others. And in doing that they can—and a good university department will have planned it so that they should—become more skilled at working in teams in a variety of roles, including leadership roles.

Why Interactive Learning?

This section treats the claims that we have just made rather more fully because they amount to a view of what higher education is for that is rather different from that which guides many people's teaching practices. In this case, fine tuning might involve some change to assumptions about what learning is for and about what learning is. That is important because there is a lot of respectable Australian research (Prosser & Trigwell, 1999) that shows three things:

1. As we said in Chapter 2, students will tend to approach an assignment with either a "deep" or a "surface" intention. The approach that students adopt is

affected by the their ideas about what counts as learning and their beliefs about what faculty expect.

2. In turn, faculty's approaches to teaching can be related to their beliefs about what counts as learning. For some, learning is amassing information, whereas for others it is about creating a sustainable personal understanding of the material.

The implication is that simply broadening the range of teaching and learning techniques in a course is not enough to improve student learning. Ideally, new techniques should be matched to an understanding that learning is about more than reproducing information (point 2); to telling students in your assessment plan and at other times that you value something more than information mastery (point 1); and to a declaration that deep approaches are welcomed.

Taking up a position like this is making a declaration about the quality of student learning. It is saying that *this* sort of learning is preferable to *that*. In fairness we need to work a word of caution in here. Your work to spread high quality learning—to encourage deep approaches—might not pay off in terms of higher grades or, even in terms of student appreciation. Higher grades might not appear because the grading system might continue to assess and reward the information mastery that is characteristic of the surface approaches that higher education can be so good at encouraging. A nasty twist is that faculty who have managed to change course assessment to reward students who take up deep approaches might see grades rise but they might also be accused of contributing to a lowering of standards and to grade inflation. Worse still, students accustomed to the certainties of the conventional grade-performance exchange, where they know the rules of the academic game and how to perform in order to get good grades, might not welcome a new deep approaches game. If it comes with an emphasis on more group work, self-directed learning and peer assessment, not only will some feel threatened but they might also start to say that the instructor's job is to instruct and ask what are they drawing their pay check for if they are laying the responsibility for learning on the students. Poorly designed student evaluation forms that are not customized for individual courses only make things worse.

Here, then, is an area where fine tuning your teaching practice might not be an easy ride, although there are many faculty who think that it is important to encourage deep approaches and to use more interactive teaching and learning methods to encourage it. There is also a lot of evidence that when students understand why this course might be different from others, then they will give it a chance. And if grades do not rise, at least there can be the consolation that performance is being sustained and that the quality of learning behind that performance is better than when non-interactive teaching is the norm.

Six reasons for making greater use of group and interactive learning methods are summarized in Box 6.1.

6.1. Seven Reasons for Adopting Interactive and Group Teaching and Learning Approaches.

1. *Active Learning.* Interactive and group learning make it hard to be a passive recipient of information. It is not impossible, but it is a lot less likely. Presumably, we want our courses to encourage the active learner (who inclines towards a deep approach to learning) not the passivity of the surface approach.

2. *Efficient Learning.* Group work enables students to take on larger and more complex research tasks than they could tackle alone. Even where topics are quite self-contained, it makes a lot of sense to distribute out the information collection work. An advantage is that having to present a summary of what has been learned to the others, who might not properly understand it, is a very good way of coming to understand something well oneself.

3. *Better Learning—Higher Order Thinking*. Edward de Bono is a world-famous proponent of methods for helping us to think better, the most famous of which is "lateral thinking." He is critical of groups, pointing out that they can be slow, cumbersome, wander off task, be dominated by the most powerful, rather than by the best thinkers, and find it impossible to make decisions. Researchers into groups in grade schools have also concluded that group work is not an efficient form of classroom organization when the aim is to complete routine and low-level tasks. These are wise criticisms and they have less significance when two other circumstances apply:

- The group is primarily a discussion forum to help individuals to think better.
- Groups are used for higher order activities, such as analysis, critical appraisal and evaluation or judgment. In grade schools, groups are particularly important in social science subjects where value issues, problems with evidence, and matters of judgment are all important.

The reason why interactions can be valuable in these areas is because they provide challenges to our views that prompt us to develop better defenses for them or to develop new views. More people get to say what they think in small groups than could ever speak to a professor, which means more people are challenged to think when they work interactively.

There are also changes to the quality of thinking. Teachers have an authority to which we tend to defer. However, when our peers challenge views, we tend to defend them more extensively and more vigorously, perhaps attacking our equals' views into the bargain. Quite simply, we are likely to think better when working with equals but to defer to our teachers.

1. **Better learning—the Zone of Proximal Development (ZPD).** "What I can do with help today I will be able to do alone tomorrow" is the principle behind the ZPD. In groups people can manage things that lie near to but a little outside their current, unaided zone of competence. Collectively, people can tackle activities that lie in the ZPD, which is the basis for learning to do those things alone in the future.

2. **Better learning—feedback and guidance.** Not only do group and interactive learning strategies ensure that students get more feedback, it is very important that it is feedback from equals. It gets considered both more and less seriously: less seriously because it is not treated with awe as the final grade from the professor is treated; more seriously because

people tend to respond to it with phrases such as "No way, because ...."; "Yes, and you're forgetting ...."; "Hey, that's a neat idea, can I borrow it and ...." Feedback from peers can also reach into areas that teachers do not have access to and that they probably should not judge even if they do have access.

3. **Motivation.** Groups motivate through peer pressure, if in no other ways. It is harder to opt out in group learning situations. The social interaction can even bring some fun into learning.

4. **Employability.** Group work is an excellent and for the most part enjoyable way to help students build interpersonal and other skills, and to display and refine qualities and attributes all of which are essential in the workplace after graduation.

Interesting research in the USA reported by Pascarella and Ternezini (1991) and by Astin (1997) reminds us that interactive learning takes place whether faculty plan it in to their courses or not, so students who live in dormitories and other university accommodation tend to show some learning outcomes more strongly than those who do not live together in an academic environment. So, even if you do not think that you can build interactive and group learning into your classes, you could do a lot worse than encourage your students to collaborate—by sharing reading tasks out with friends, through arranging to have coffee breaks with friends to talk over assignments, or, if you have them, through contributing to class bulletin boards or joining in on-line class conferences. Obviously, you would want to take some time to make a distinction between collaboration and plagiarism (see also Chapter 9) and it is a good idea to write it into your course syllabus or handbook as well. You might also invite groups of students to propose to you that they do collaborative assignments—the procedures in Box 6.3 can be used in allocating the marks.

Because we are convinced of the value of interactive work the rest of this chapter concentrates on ways in which you can deliberately use group and other interactive learning techniques in your course. As always, the best advice is to pick one that looks easy to introduce, use it, modify it and then look for another to try.

Types of Grouping for Interactive Learning

Groupings will often involve students talking with one or two people near to them during a presentation. Once they have agreed on a view on the problem set by the instructor they might be told to turn in their seats and check out their answer with one or two others within speaking distance. The groups are short-lived. At the other extreme are Action Learning Sets (ALSs) which are groups that last throughout a course or a program. Together the members of ALSs share reading, web and library searching, assignment planning, writing, presenting, and the important business of supporting each other emotionally in difficult and dank times.

Just as groups can have a half life measured in minutes or become a regular learning family, so too they can number from two to about 20, including perhaps a seminar leader for larger groups. Most educators probably feel that while a group can be too large to be effective, there is less agreement on how large is too large. Osborne (1983) describes successful adult learning study circles of up to 20 participants. In groups of five to eight, Weisberg, Knapper, and Wilcox (1996) reported two people will regularly make a disproportionate contribution. And Feichtner and Davis (1985) believe that groups can also be too small, recommending a number between four and seven.

We have thought about this quite a bit and conclude that an effective group size will probably depend on the type of group tasks assigned and the size of the class. So, two students assigned to work together on a project form the simplest and smallest type of group. In any partnership, which is what this is, personal compatibility is an important feature. Uneven ability levels can be a problem if one student surrenders initiative for the work to the other, although this can lead to the dominant partner learning better through needing to teach the other so much. The ideal partnership is seldom found except for short periods of time and in specific circumstances. It is not well suited to in-depth discussion tasks.

Three students can form a good project-working group, and might also form a good discussion group, although an intense dialogue with the third student left out is always a danger. We are a group of three and we find the number appropriate for a research endeavor where we need a balance between variety of viewpoints and reasonable consensus.

Large and complex projects might benefit from a team of four students, although seldom more. Four students, or more, up to about seven or eight, form a good size for discussions: in general, the longer the time allocated to discussion, the larger a group can be. We suggest a short discussion of ten minutes is good for four students, while a group of eight students would require more than twice that time for each to have their say.

When it comes to group composition, different approaches suit different purposes. Robert tends to arrange groupings and to do it alphabetically. And it is not difficult to see why he prefers to assign students to groups simply on the basis of their order in the class registration list: he teaches classes of almost 200 students where simplicity saves time and decreases work. When he is pressed further: Peter asks him "What do you do if there are four Smiths or three Wongs, both sets of siblings?" Of course, Robert reassigns these students to other groups whether they are related or not, such that each group member has a different surname. "What do you do if two of them don't get along?" asks Nola. "Immediate, no-questions-asked reassignment to another group" replies Robert, adding "I find a no-investigation, no-blame, no-reprisal approach is most appreciated by students when problems arise. Treat them both as adults." Some faculty go so far as to say that in real life we have to work with difficult colleagues and that assigning people to groups is one way of giving them experience that anticipates real life work situations. Others feel that letting students form their own groups means that they are likely to form groups that will work, which is fairest because it gives them all the best chance of performing well. Viewed in this way it seems that an important variable is whether there is high stakes assessment attached to the group task. If there is, it will be harder to defend any grouping that stops people working with their preferred partners.

In a long-term grouping such as an ALS it is important that group members negotiate and renegotiate their own roles, always recognizing that these roles will be and will have to be fluid. In other cases groups are formed to complete a well-defined assignment in a relatively short time and it often helps matters to say that each group should identify someone to fill each of the following roles.

- a noise monitor who tells people to keep the noise down
- a turn-taking monitor who makes sure no-one hogs the discussion
- a seating monitor, alert to anyone who is seated too far away to hear or participate in the discussion
- a writer or person who fills in the answer sheet
- a discussion leader, chair, or referee
- a librarian who looks things up
- a summarizer who tries to bring closure to any discussion

Roles might be rotated at each meeting.

Making the Class Buzz

These nine classroom-tested group structures can be modified to suit your needs. It does not take long to find your favorites and have students ask for them. To ensure that they work smoothly, it is very important that the students (and you) know why you are doing them and understand the procedure well. Sometimes it takes a couple of shots to get them rolling, so be prepared to persevere. Depending on your situation, some will work better than others, so be prepared also to let it go if it is clearly not working or the students are just not on board.

One general point is that all of these activities work best if they are not a snapshot pooling of ignorance. Either set preparation work before the class or say that you are shortly going to ask students to comment, offer a view or take a position on something and tell them to think about what they will say and why, summing it up in no more than 25 words of notes. Give them up to two minutes and then move into the activities.

1. Buzz Groups, Pairs, or Triads

This works well as a warmer at the beginning of your class—particularly good on Monday mornings.

1. Give a question on whatever the topic or reading you are working on to subgroups of 2 to 4 students.
2. You or the subgroup members choose a leader for each subgroup to record and report the important ideas to the whole group.
3. Students "buzz" for five minutes while you jolly and prod reluctant buzzers along, or be a devil's advocate to others, etc.
4. Leaders take turns to report three of the most important points of their group to the whole class.
5. You record those three from each group to further the discussion or use as a starting off point for the next class.
6. Stages 4 and 5 will have to be missed with large classes. Instead, treat the "buzzing" as preparation for the next stage of the presentation, as shown in Box 5. 1.

2. Pyramids (or Think/Write-Pair-Share)

In this group structure students work alone, then in pairs, then fours, sixes, and finally as a whole group. Students do an individual activity first such as reading for information or solving a problem. They think the task through—take some notes, and then share with the person next to them. The pair comes up with new ideas and it snowballs from there when they pair with a nearby pair. Ideas are pooled and it can snowball to three pairs or more. This is more time consuming but it does allow in-depth learning and understanding and a surprising amount of material can be covered in active participation such as this.

3. Debates

This is similar to the usual debate but this one has total involvement at certain parts of the structure.

1. Divide the class into sides of pro and con by an imaginary line though the center of the classroom. If you have a class of 100 students, have them get into groups of 4-5.
2. Each small group comes up with the pros and a prepared rebuttal for some cons to an issue and the other half of the class in small groups does the similar thing except prepares for the cons.
3. At a designated time, (about ten minutes) the class debates the issue.
4. For each point the side makes, have a designated student rack it up for that side. If it is refuted, the team loses the point.

This can get rowdy, but if it is well done, it is a hit. (While many students don't get to speak in the whole class part, the real work and active learning took place in the groups of four—the rest is sport.)

---

4. Crossovers

Both pyramids and debates hit reporting back problems when classes are medium-sized or large. Unless you are in a tiered lecture theater (when techniques like that in Box 5.1 should be used), try crossovers.

1. Small groups reach a position on an issue, problem or whatever.
2. Each person in a group has a number (1-4 in groups of four, 1-5 in groups of five, and so on).
3. All number 5s assemble in one part of the hall, all number 4s in another, and so on. They reform into new groups of four or five.
4. The new groups rework the original question. Each group, of course, contains people who have already done this in different groups. In effect, they are each reporting back to a small audience of people who constitute an informed and perhaps sceptical audience.

5. Rounds

This is a good icebreaker and gets the reluctant speaker speaking up in a small class, and works best if students sit in a circle. Each student must take a turn at saying something. To get the ball rolling, use prompts such as "A question I'd like to know the answer to today is …." As soon as students have spoken once in class, they are more likely to feel comfortable to speak up again later. This works well at the beginning of the semester when students do not know each other and are reluctant to speak up and share their ideas and concerns.

6. Fishbowls

This is so named because of the physical shape it takes. It consists of two concentric circles; one small circle comprising the half-dozen or so students who will have the discussion, and the larger one comprising the remainder of the students who will listen in. The students in the center circle discuss an issue and give their perspective; solve a problem, discuss a case study, etc. Those in the outer circle can "tap in" to the inner circle by tapping one of the students on the shoulder and replacing him or her. This also can get hectic, but the advantage is that the students have control of the discussion and when they have heard enough from one speaker, they can take him/her out!

7. Silent Brainstorming

This is variation of the more well known brainstorm activity. In this one, students are in groups of 4-6 and each has a sheet of paper. They are given a common problem to solve or issue to expand, etc., similar to a regular brainstorm. The difference here is that everyone is guaranteed to be involved because they all share their ideas.

---

1. To start, they write one idea or solution on the paper.
2. Once done, they pass the paper to the left and take the person's paper from the right. They read the person's idea and must come up with a different one. They can "hitchhike" if it is an improvement or development of the idea, but usually have to come up with something fresh.
3. Next they pass their paper to the person directly opposite and take that person's paper and repeat.
4. At this point, you should be able to tell if students have enough ideas to go again, this time passing to the right.
5. Continue until the students are almost drained of ideas. You will notice that this is a more comfortable brainstorm session for shy students or students who think their ideas do not have merit.
6. You can either leave things there, or have groups prepare a brief report that you read, or collect the papers and while the class does something else or goes on a break, produce a rough and ready list on the OHP of main points and use this as a starting point in the next part of the class. See also Box 5.1.

8. Poster Tours

Have you ever noticed that after small discussions where a recorder records ideas on chart paper, or the members illustrate the issue in some way in poster fashion, that the activity is all downhill from there? Certainly the small group process is one of the best for getting students to be active learners and thinkers, but the small groups only get to share about three of their most important ideas in the plenary discussion. A poster tour will ensure that students will get to more of the groups' discussion points effectively and efficiently. Box 7.8 shows how the posters can be marked.

1. Have students in small groups work on a poster to illustrate the most important points of their discussion of a set topic.
2. Have one student stay with the poster to answer questions as the others make the tour of the class posters.
3. Once the tour is over, the students who stood by the poster have their tour while each group writes on cards comments or additional questions about the posters and leave at each poster station. The comment cards act as a springboard to continue the discussion to the next class and develop your content from there.

9. Jigsaw

This is quick and fairly effective way to cover a lot of information.

1. In this group structure, arrange about four students to a "home group."
2. The students leave their home group and go to topic stations in the room

and work in newly formed groups at the station to master material and become "experts" on the topic that you have set. Your job is to circulate among the stations to ensure that the expert groups understand the material and can communicate it to others accurately.

3. Next, each student from the expert groups returns to his or her home group. In the home group each expert teaches the experts of their topic in turn.
4. When each of the experts has done that, they use the new knowledge to solve a problem or do some other related activity right away or leave to open it up in the next class.

Group Learning Projects

Group organization is not a fix for dull learning activities. Dreary assignments are still dreary even if the boredom is shared around a group. This section contains six ideas for interactive work that is likely to be livelier and to lead to deep approaches to learning.

1. Classroom Discussion

We have already suggested that it is a feature of good pedagogy for a university teacher to pause after fifteen minutes of lecturing and ask students to discuss something for five minutes. This might be as simple as "turn to your neighbor," or it might be possible to form larger groups and include crossovers.

Sometimes it is a good idea to build up group confidence by asking something for which there is a certain answer, rather than some more complex question which might keep them puzzled for weeks. This is particularly important if the same group meets for discussion for several classes.

It is often difficult to bring a discussion period to a conclusion, but if the teacher circulates during the discussion, he or she will likely overhear one or two interesting views that can be used for illustration. Without giving the answer the teacher can broaden the discussion to the whole class by asking individuals to express their view and then by asking how many groups considered this. It is of course important that the teacher maintains control over the discussion and moves quickly to prevent or subdue any insult or severe criticism of any student that might emerge.

2. Classroom Group Tests

In large classroom situations, particularly where testing is frequent and computer-scored, it is possible to re-humanize the experience for students by allowing a group to do the test. You might have individual testing first. Then allow the students to discuss the test in groups and agree on a group answer. This is a form of feedback to all students, allowing them to argue and reason for a simple choice, and if you wish, to look up the relevant information in a textbook.

3. Practical Classroom Work

Practical classroom work is likely to take one of three forms: reading/writing groups, "dry" laboratory groups (using maps, drawing equipment, computers) and "wet" laboratory groups (using glassware, chemicals, samples, instruments).

Peer tutoring can be a useful form of reading/writing group activity that can benefit both tutors and tutored. It requires that the tutors have some previous instruction on helping the tutored to write, which might or might not be possible in your own situation. The purpose of a peer writing or reading group, however formed, will be to provide critical appraisal and help by peers. Whether it occurs in a language class or in some other branch of the humanities and social sciences, students are less likely to be ashamed of their deficiencies if they are sharing their writing with each other, rather than with the teacher or in front of the whole class.

Groups function well in dry laboratories, but are always more efficient if kept small: two or three students is the best size, especially if there are maps or other large documents to handle and spread out, or boxes of samples to be examined. A larger group might work if each group can be assigned a separate table that they can comfortably sit around. Computer labs are a special case. When dealing with computer novices it is always best that they work in pairs. More advanced students should either work individually or in larger groups where the computer is but one tool used in a research project.

In wet laboratories the optimal group is a pair. Safety concerns will tend to restrict group size when wet-laboratory equipment is used, following the kitchen wisdom of "too many cooks spoil the broth." Certain specialized labs such as dissecting a human or large animal cadaver might work well with groups of up to four students with good results and little danger.

4. Fieldwork

Fieldwork is a special kind of practical experience where, because it is outside the classroom, security or safety is an important issue. Students should always work in pairs or groups of up to four, whether their activities take place in an urban, rural or wilderness setting, whether they are involved in interviewing or using instruments to survey or sample the ground. Because fieldwork is often such an intensely pleasurable social experience, there will always be a tendency for groups to self-select into groups of friends. You must be alert to recognize whether such groups are well-balanced or not, whether they would be distracted from the activity and develop another agenda (boy and girlfriend as a pair), whether they are sufficiently heterogeneous in terms of ability levels, and whether there is at least one "steady" person in each group: someone to remind them in the euphoria of being out of class or away in the wilderness, that there is an academic purpose to the activity!

5. Research and Presentation Groups

Research projects which require use of library or electronic resources, perhaps some collecting of original data and analysis, and typically result in an essay, report or live presentation, are a feature of a great many disciplines. Robert is particularly keen on having his groups create a poster that can be displayed in a poster session where some peer evaluation is possible. Group work allows students to take on more ambitious projects which might be simply too demanding for an individual, or require too much time. In such group projects, teamwork and cooperative skills are developed. It is very important that students are required to plan and carefully divide up the work and the costs of materials or other expenses, and share these equally. Because students often complain that too much work is assigned after class, and that meeting as a group after class is difficult because of schedules, jobs and other commitments, it is often a good idea to schedule some class time for group meetings, even allowing the groups to leave the classroom as a group. To be sure that students stay on schedule, it makes sense to expect them to submit an outline of the project and an interim report on progress.

Live presentation by a group should always involve all members, even though one might be very shy and another a complete extrovert. Try to get the idea across that they are a team: one might be a star, but the whole team must be prepared to perform to the best of their ability. While the extrovert will enjoy performing, the shy one will probably gain more from the experience, and see it as an opportunity to improve in an area that they know only too well needs improvement.

6. Electronic Interaction

We leave to one side those electronic interactions that can happen as you sail around the web and make inquiries of people whose work you locate through the Internet. That is not to say that they are unimportant, for we all learn a lot by following up messages on bulletin boards, responding to E-mail inquiries and simply asking networks if they can offer help or advice. It is therefore right to encourage students to use their ICT skills to interact in these ways. But here the main concern is what faculty can do to encourage electronic interaction amongst the class, to promote the development of vibrant "virtual communities." Agreed, there is no substitute for face-to-face interaction and class meetings provide a lot of opportunities for this that can be extended by people choosing to meet and talk and work over coffee. Box 6.2 gives some of the advantages of planned electronic interactions, suggesting that sometimes virtual communities are necessary (for distance learning students) and at other times there are ways in which virtual communities complement face-to-face interactions. Box 3.5 looked at ICT usage in more general terms.

6.2. *Advantages of Planned Electronic Interactions*

- They suit many part-time students and those who live off campus who cannot do informal, face-to-face networking. (However, there is an equity issue here, since not all homes have PCs and outside North America phone tolls are expensive enough to deter Internet usage).
- These interactions are necessary for those taking their degrees by distance learning.
- Many communications packages support asynchronous interaction: I log on and contribute to a web discussion and you log on and contribute later. In some ways this is far more flexible as a means of interaction than scheduled synchronous sessions, such as video conferencing.
- Extended asynchronous interactions are possible without the fatigue that would come if they were all crammed into face-to-face work.
- You have a record of all the contributions that can be consulted, thought about, and even edited into an (acknowledged) part of a report or paper. In face-to-face interaction, so much gets lost.
- Where productivity and communications software are used in a group project, then they support scheduling, dialogue, editing and revisions, and project management in general.
- Extended multi-participant simulations and gaming can be done through electronic media. It would be hard to schedule them by other means and impossible to run simulations or games of such complexity and length.

When people have to interact as virtual communities, they do. Many, though, have a preference for face-to-face interaction and, at the time of writing, remain reluctant to do interact *for work purposes* through communications technologies. In part that is because it is not usual for higher education courses to have their own electronic conferences, or interactive sites. It is also often more satisfying for the student to approach the teacher at the end of a class than it is to send off an E-mail. In part this is because face-to-face communication is the best way to check out that the other person does understand what you are asking or getting at. With asynchronous communication, such as E-mail, it can take a lot of to-ing and fro-ing to get confusions sorted. With video conferencing things are better but still inferior to face-to-face communication.

Electronic interactions are valuable. Without them, this book, which was started face-to-face, would never have been completed. Their importance is still emerging.

Grading Group Projects

Where learning to work in groups is a course outcome you are likely to want to (a) have some assignments or exams done in groups, and (b) to reward skill as a group or team member. The second of these points is contentious because you could say that it is only the other group members who know enough to judge each other's skill in teamwork. There are difficulties, then, in getting this skill graded, since it would be difficult to be sure that the peer-assessments on which you would be dependent would be reliable. There is no reason why these peer judgments could not be made on a formative, low-stakes basis but there are all sorts of problems if they are to have any high stakes function.

It is much easier to set and grade group assignments and group exams. For example, a group exam is written in small groups or pairs usually at home in students' own time. The kind of questions you give are not retrieval-based, but should be questions that seek higher levels of understanding such as synthesis and evaluation. The group discussion and argument that arise during this examination can be valuable as learning in their own right and should mean that deep approaches and higher level thinking come into play. The exam becomes another learning experience where students can use references and pooled resources that are unavailable during a traditional exam. This lower-stress exam is popular among our students. They have to agree up-front, however, to accept the system that is going to be used for getting individual marks from a group exam or assignment. Box 6.3 (p. 112) shows several ways of doing this. A procedure for running group exams is in Box 6.4 (p. 113).

Finding Out More

An excellent reference is *Teaching More Students: Discussion with More Students*, from the Instructional Development Center at Queens' University in Kingston, Ontario. Go to http://www.queensu.ca/idc/HandBook/semtut.html and check out their Alternative Instructional Methods.

You can also quite easily adapt for adult learners some well-tried ideas from grade school. Good sources of ideas are Johnson, Johnson & Holubec's *Cooperative Learning in the Classroom* and Kagan's *Cooperative Learning*.

6.3. Ways of Getting Individual Marks from Group Exams and As-signments.

1. Life can be tough: Everyone gets the group mark.

In real life a group has to deliver. If not everyone gets blamed—easy riders and superheroes alike. The same is true for praise when it succeeds.

In this approach students are told that this is a test of how well they pull together in a group (and they probably have not had a choice of which group they're going to work in) and so they all get the group mark.

Example: group mark = 76%; each student gets 76%. No complaining allowed.

2. No easy riders.

There are several methods for stopping people hitching a free ride on others' efforts. One, mentioned above, is simply to remove them from the group if there are complaints and to have them submit an individual piece of work.

The other is to have all students complete a peer-evaluation that is sealed in an envelope and handed in with the project. Typically, they are asked to rate the contribution that each has made to the project. Some evaluations use several evaluative categories, although the following example is more common:

> Please write the names of each person in the group who did this project, including yourself, and rate each one on this five point scale that shows their commitment to getting it done.
>
> 1 = Worked really hard on this, far more than anyone else
> 2 = Did their share
> 3 = OK
> 4 = Didn't do as much as everyone else but made some effort
> 5 = Who are we talking about?

The rule is that anyone who gets, say, two 5s gets a pre-specified penalty perhaps a 30% deduction from the group mark. It could be extended to impose lesser penalties on people getting 4s from fellow students.

Example. Three students get 76%. One gets 46%.

3. Mathematical sophistication

Again, students rate each other's efforts. This time a calculation is done to estimate each person's relative commitment. Suppose there are four people in the group and that the mean rating for each are 4.3, 4.1, 3.9 and 3.6. These are in the same ball park and the obvious thing is to let the group mark stand for each. But what if the ratings are 4.5, 4.0, 3.5 and 3.0?

First, decide whether you are going to adjust the whole mark (76%, remember), or to take a second scenario, just a portion of it (say, 30 of the marks). Then find the mean of the four ratings (3.75) and calculate how many *percent* above or below that mean each individual rating is (+0.2, +0.067; - 0.067; -0.2). Now raise or lower the marks accordingly (76 x 1.2; 76 x 1.067; 76 x 0.933; 76 x 0.8. Or, in the second scenario, multiply 30 by 1.2, 1.067, 0.933, 0.8 and add the products to each student's core mark of 46%).

Both methods spread the marks out: Where all 76 marks are redistributed the range is now from 91% to 61%. Where just 30 marks are recalculated the range is now from 82% to 70%.

The big question is whether it is worth the effort. Box 4.6 contained the suggestion that outlying marks should first be discarded.

6.4. Organizing a Group Exam

1. Assign groups ahead of time. A good way is to number students off so that the randomness allows for knowledge, skill, and group dynamics. Self-selected groups can be uncomfortable for some students, unfair to most and stressful in their own right.

2. Give the students the questions and the time in which the common paper must be handed in. Remind them to work to bring out, organize and combine their individual strengths. In an ideal situation some students might be strong in understanding and articulating the question and efficient at locating information, another might be good at sifting through and analyzing it. Another good at synthesizing the main points, while another communicates well. However, sometimes some students work better doing this collaboratively instead of delegating tasks.

3. Make it clear how grading will be done, both in terms of grading criteria or rubrics and mark distribution procedures (Box 6.2).

4. Tell students what to do in the emergency that *will* happen—if someone gets sick, misses a plane, throws a panic attack. The longer the time available to do the exam the more these emergency plans are needed.

7. Working with Large Classes

Preview

Good teaching is good teaching, irrespective of class size. Six principles for working with large classes are:

* What's good for small classes is good for large ones
* Be well prepared and explicit
* Look at all of the learning arrangements
* Encourage collaboration and group formation
* Look for efficient assessments
* Listen

The Problems

The scene is a fresh, early September morning. Two faculty members meet, walking across campus in the same direction:

Chris: Hi Robin, off to class?
Robin: First one of the semester: exciting!
Chris: Where are you teaching, not in PE244 are you?
Robin: Yes I am. A full class too—all 180 seats occupied, and probably a few sitting on the steps too, hoping they can add the course if someone drops.
Chris: I can't stand teaching large classes: it's such a drag. You don't get to know any of the students well: you just feel you're lecturing to a great anonymous mob. No real contact; no real feedback. Just a massive load of marking.
Robin: Chris, I know what you're saying, but it needn't be that way. Good teaching is good teaching: what holds true for small classes also holds true, to a considerable extent, for large ones. Sometimes it seems that the task is more difficult, but maybe that's because we expect it to be. There are lots of techniques available to help ease the problems, although I tend to favor a more radical reworking of a course. I like to design-in effective practices rather than just bolt them on.

What are you doing right now? Why don't you come to class with me: it is easier to show you what I do than it is to explain. Come on; try something new....

Are you a Chris or a Robin? Or somewhere in between? Do you find that teaching a large class, however you might define it, is a grim experience? Do you feel frustrated at the difficulty of creating an authentic learning environment when dealing with large groups? Or maybe you are dissatisfied with your own performance in a large classroom, or with the students' performance. "Yes" to any of these and this has been written for you. There is some real potential for creating an excellent learning environment in large classrooms; you just have to learn how to arrange it.

But first, what are "large classes"?

One person's large class is another's bread and butter. There is no agreed definition of a large class, nor should there be. Signs that this is a "large class" can be:

- The class is significantly larger than you are used to
- You feel that you no longer know the students
- The grading load is getting out of control.

Now, if there is a team working on a course, or if there are some TAs or laboratory demonstrators, a class that is far too big for one person might be quite comfortable: students go to large presentations (lectures) but do lab, field, and tutorial work in smaller groups, where the instructor knows them and where they have a point of contact when queries arise. To give an example, a social science lecturer who works alone with a class of 40-50 and who grades students on course work essays and essay examinations finds this to be a large class. However, a statistics lecturer does not think 50 students makes for a large class. So, lectures aside, whether something feels like a large class is partly a matter of the resources put into teaching it.

So, let us say that a large class is one that feels large and that a sign of this will often be that you feel that the size of the class stops you from working in your preferred way.

Principle 1: What's Good for Small Classes Is Good for Large Ones

Box 7.1 lists a number of the features of large classes that can hinder the approaches to teaching and learning that have been described in previous chapters. We have accumulated quite a bit of evidence that it is possible to preserve the spirit of those approaches even in classes of hundreds. It is possible for there to be excellent learning and good teaching in large classes: the principles do not change but the pragmatics do. For example, data from large enrollment Geography classes at the University of Lethbridge clearly indicate that students perform better in a course that has high levels of student involvement and activity (and fewer formal lectures/presentations) than in a conventional "lectures then exam" arrangement. There are still more Bs than As, but there are far fewer Cs and Ds and Fs: the attainment curve has shifted to the left and shows that there has been a decided improvement even though teaching is in a large class.

7.1. Large Class Problems

- Students become faces instead of people.
- It is hard for lecturers to convey their care for and commitment to students.
- It is harder to give individual advice and guidance to students.
- Large classes might involve faculty working in teams. This might be an unfamiliar experience. There are reports that not all team members contribute equally.
- Organizational problems are compounded, making it difficult to schedule tutorials, laboratory sessions, and fieldwork.
- Professors have less flexibility.
- There can be technical problems working with large classes – inadequate microphones, difficulties in projecting slides that are clearly visible, inadequate OHPs.
- Some academic staff feel intimidated when facing an unbroken array of faces.
- Some tutors fear greater control problems.
- It can be impossible to monitor attendance.
- There is a feeling that you need to be a charismatic performer to work with large classes.
- Coping with large numbers of assignments and examination scripts is a source of difficulty.
- The quality of feedback to students can be much reduced in large classes.

In large classes neither the learning nor the teaching techniques are, in essence, special. What is special is the planning that allows good learning and teaching to flourish in a logistically-hostile environment in which improvisation is riskier and individualized troubleshooting is virtually impossible. So, the principles for good presentations that were described in Chapter 5 are the same when the class is large—the main differences will be that the presenter will be wearing a clip-on microphone (*never* standing at a lectern speaking into a fixed mike) and that with very large groups it might not be physically possible to move into the audience. If, as a presenter, you have a style that meets the guidelines in Box 7.2, then the class size is pretty irrelevant.

7.2. Good Presentational Style For Large And Small Classes.

- Involves a relaxed posture.
- Does not involve reading from notes but which is closer to a conversation with the audience.
- Has plenty of eye contact with learners from all parts of the room.
- Shows good body language at work—the use of the hands and arms is important here, especially movements that draw learners in to the presentation.
- Uses a variety of voice levels and pitches, and not a voice that is marked by fast, monotone, or one-pace talking.
- Uses clear visual aids: video, computer display or overhead transparency slides that have been checked out by someone standing at the back of the room and concentrating on the smallest typeface used.

Principle 2: Be Well Prepared and Be Explicit

In Chapter 3 we suggested that a version of the course syllabus could be shared with students in the form of a course handbook. In Chapter 4 we said that fair assessment practice involved sharing with students the criteria or marking rubrics that would apply to high stakes assessments, and Chapter 5 referred to the value of introductions that comprise the presentation's headline points. With large classes it is even more important that students have this clarity because uncertainties and confusions are simply harder to deal with when there are so many people involved—and the effects of a couple of hundred confused or unhappy students can be a lot more noticeable than those of half-a-dozen. Box 7.3 contains one teacher's advice on being clear.

7.3. On Being Clear with a Large Class

Take time with a large class to explain it all comprehensively and to field questions on the conduct of the class. That can come at the back end of the first meeting (the front end should be more alluring and academically important). When you have a large class, the number of students who might miss something presented orally, or who might be absent on some occasion, is of course far greater than in a small class. You do not want to be bogged down by their requests for interpreting the elementary, so you make everything as clear and unambiguous as possible and to give it to them in print (and perhaps put it on the web as well).

If you combine a strict schedule (published in the course handbook or syllabus) with a course text, then those who miss a session can easily make up some of the ground without troubling you. Most large-enrollment introductory classes, particularly those in the sciences, have a required text. The character referred to as Robin in the opening dialogue uses a text written by an experienced faculty member from a college 3000 km away. Robin has found that it is best to stick to the order of chapters used in the text. While this practice is not recommended in small classes because it does not allow for spontaneity, not take into account students' interests and needs at the time, it seems a more manageable way to deal with large classes. Lots of the material introduced by the teacher might be different from the material in the text, for instance you might provide local examples to those phenomena described in the text, but the same order is used. Three years ago Robin used a different text which had a different order of treatment and so the course back then was different, not in total scope and content, but in the order that each topic was presented. And it will change again, unless the next textbook adopted coincides in order of presentation to the present one. The students of course appreciate this very linear approach to textbook use: they always know where they are in the course, even if they miss some time due to illness or other reason: catching up is relatively straightforward.

Tell students where they will be able to get spare handouts and other course materials (on your web site, perhaps) so that you are not victim of endless requests for copies.

We would add one other point. It reassures students if they know how you are approaching this course with such a large class. The approach recommended here has six principles to it. If students know what they are, then they are better placed to follow your lead. An example of one patter is in Box 7.4.

7.4. Setting Out Some Principles For Taking A Large Class

Your learning is what this course is all about. My job is to do everything I can to make that learning possible. Face-to-face teaching is an important part of it but it's not the only part. For instance, for every hour you spend in a class with me you'll spend about another eight hours working on this course alone or with others, in the library, in your dorm, or wherever. So, it's important that I make sure that you have good readings, good activities and assignments and that you get to share your learning with each other as well as with me. The size of this class doesn't make it any harder for me to plan for you to have good learning.

In this class I shall follow the sequence that is in course handbook, which also tells you what the assignments and tests will be, and how they will be marked. It also tells you how to make up any ground that you lose through absence.

I shall do one presentation each week in which I will be mainly concerned with setting up a framework for organizing the material covered in that week's reading, or for making sense of a controversy or problematic issue.

Because a lot of information is in the textbook and in the other readings that I have identified, I can expect you to add information to the frameworks that I set up in the presentations. That is one of your main jobs: to make sure you have notes of the information you need on each week's topic. I will not dictate notes, nor give lectures that do nothing except tell you what you can read in the textbook. You, then, are responsible for getting the information to flesh out the frameworks I will construct in the presentations.

The other sessions will be ones in which you will be working in smaller groups on activities that should extend your understanding, require you to apply ideas and techniques, and sometimes involve you changing them. They will not be like conventional classes because the assumption will be that you are well enough prepared to get on with applying your knowledge to the problems, issues and other tasks that you will face. Details of these activities are also in the handbook.

If you have difficulty with any of the material, the first step should be to talk about it with other people on the course. If they are stuck, or if you still do not understand it, let me know. The best way to do that is to post a question to the course conference on the web but you are welcome to E-mail me or to leave me a note.

Behind both of these points is the obvious one that really good preparation is needed to run good large classes. That does not just mean having slick presentations, although they always help. It means having planned all the details of the complete student learning package. Remember, they will spend much more time learning when you are not with them than they will in face-to-face contact with you, which is why it is so important to look at what you intend the students to do, not just at the performances you intend to give.

Principle 3: Look at All of The Learning Arrangements

In content-intensive courses, which are common in the early stages of any degree program when large classes are endemic, it is tempting to move at a rapid pace through as much of the material as possible, resorting to rapid-fire lectures and to keep exchanges between teacher and students to a minimum. This must be resisted if you are to be successful in helping the students to understand the subject you are teaching. Coverage must be sacrificed for understanding, and lectures must be reduced in number or "intensity" to allow time for other kinds of learning activities. Most courses at the university level involve two or three meetings per week designated as "lectures." In addition there might be a block of time for laboratory work, and very rarely some time set aside for tutorials and small group work. The prospect of working with a mass audience is likely to make the teacher think in terms of delivering a message to them and to blank out the notion that there could be interaction between students and audience participation. Our view is that student learning is best helped if we do not fill all of the designated lecture slots with presentations. Although many university courses remain 100% lectures there are estimates that students will learn only 10 to 20% of the material presented in a lecture, there is also an estimate that the percentage doubles if they are involved in the simple act of discussing the material with others. For the sake of learning efficiency it makes sense to have discussions or experiential learning during the class meetings.

One way to ensure that students are keeping up with the material is to assign reading every week, and promise that at least part of the evaluation will focus on the material that is read. It is a very good idea to help guide their reading by setting them questions to answer. Some texts come with them ready-made at the end of each chapter. Alternatively, you might introduce questions that require the application or extension of the concepts to fresh material. In that case construct questions which derive from an *understanding* of each, not just memorizing content, nor simply the same questions. Sometimes the questions in the texts are information-grabbing ones and you might decide to displace them with yours which are designed to be more thought-provoking and better stimuli to understanding.

This emphasis on out-of-class learning can be consolidated by planned interactive work. Sometimes it is useful to tell students to arrange to meet with each other in groups and at times that suit them and to discuss, analyze, criticize, or evaluate a topic of your choice.

Principle 4: Encourage Collaboration and Group Formation

Organizing a large class into discussion groups is not easy, and sometimes the sheer difficulty of the task deters teachers from trying. For instance, you might teach in a ramped lecture theater with fixed seats and fixed, continuous, long tables. Yet even in such a classroom, very successful discussions in groups of four to six students can take place if two or three people on one row turn to talk with those behind them. Chapter 6 gave fuller advice on interactive techniques that can then be used

If the classroom is a flat one with moveable tables and chairs, then there are all sorts of possibilities, including some quite complex pyramiding and crossover arrangements (see Chapter 6). Another idea is that at the first class meeting, you should ask the students to refer to a list posted outside the classroom that allocates them to small discussion groups. Five minutes before the second class, you dash into the room and stick "post-it" notes on the seats: 6 (or however many you determine are in a group) for group A; 6 for group B; and so on to group Z or beyond (AA, BB etc. after Z) depending on class size. When the students enter the class, each student sits at a seat marked with the group listed next to his or her name on the list outside. In a very short time, the class is organized into the groups with relatively little confusion. Have many groups of five or six rather than fewer, larger groups; more small groups means that more students get to speak (and to think) more and for longer.

Sure, it can get noisy, although appointing noise monitors in each group will help (see Chapter 6). Certainly it will seem chaotic at times, but the chaos is more likely productive than destructive to good learning, and in the opinion of most experienced and successful university teachers, far better as a learning environment than the quiet orderly class which listens to a lecture at every meeting.

In some courses there is provision for regular tutorials or small group meetings with a teacher or TA. Whatever the learning value of these scheduled groups, they are also important for helping students to identify with the class, the course and the department. They get to meet and work with the same people regularly and they identify a teacher who they can turn to with academic concerns and with nonacademic problems. Arrangements like these are extremely important for freshman students, who are the most likely to feel overwhelmed because they only attend large classes, often unnoticed by anyone. Box 7.5 contains some guidelines for running tutorial groups.

Any other ways that can be found to help students in large classes to make contact with each other are worth pursuing as ways of reducing the potential for alienation and anonymity, as well as because interactions are opportunities for learning. For example, use icebreakers, such as the one in Box 7.6 (p. 122)

Other teachers might prefer to get students to interview each other, or simply orally introduce themselves to their neighbors.

Principle 5: Look for Efficient Assessments

If you have decided to adopt an "activity-based" teaching style where students will contribute to their own learning in a cooperative fashion, you will have to consider frequent testing of some form, so that individuals and groups develop

7.5. Pointers For Tutorials And Other Small Groups.

By definition, small group teaching—tutorials, laboratory work, practical classes, work-place attachments, and fieldwork—does not have the same problems as are raised by large classes. Yet, what counts as a small group can still be quite large, with 30, 40, or more students. Untrained people should not really be given responsibility for such groups, particularly because these groups offer important opportunities to do things that cannot be done with larger groups but which need a skilled teacher if they are to work. Where a number of TAs all work on the same course, it is a good idea to have them meet regularly, think about suitable pedagogies for the next run of small group meetings, and pay them for doing so.

- Make sure that the small group tutor has it as a priority to learn students' names and to help them to learn each other's names. If students can identify with the course through those sessions, it can help to dispel feelings of anonymity and alienation that can flow from the scale of large lecture classes.
- Realize that this is a good opportunity for students to raise questions – things they don't understand, course issues, procedural matters.
- Provide opportunities for small group work.
- Recall that in many subjects, these are the session in which students should be evaluating, applying, analyzing, criticizing, and synthesizing the information and insights they have gained from presentations and reading. These sessions *must* be ones that are mentally demanding.
- Monitor performance and give useful feedback on it (see also the section on assessment, overleaf).
- Consider the implication that TAs and others who take these classes need training; often, for example, they need to learn to listen, to re-direct questions, re-frame them, to prompt, clarify, pose questions, and to summarize. These skills might be at the expense of more didactic impulses.
- Likewise, the course team or leader would be well advised to plan an outline of the small group sessions with as much care as the large presentations are planned.

some awareness of progress in the construction of knowledge. It is not a bad idea to examine students almost every week. Usually ten questions suffice. If each test is worth 4% of the course grade, then ten tests would accumulate 40% of the final mark. Assuming that these are mainly tests of knowledge, that would allow 60% of the marks to be based on activities that demanded more by way of higher order mental processes.

Without the use of ICT, frequent testing of a large class would be impractical. Computer-scored sheets provide a very appropriate way to perform most test marking. This requires that the tests are constructed in a selected-response format. Where these tests of knowledge are one component of the assessment of student learning, then that can be justified; Box 4.1 contained an assessment plan in which the assessment of knowledge was a clear component. One effective and simple way to avoid the rote-learning syndrome is to ask questions that require students to identify the one correct or incorrect statement out of four alternatives. This places emphasis on student understanding, not memorization of terms.

Other ways of reducing the assessment load have been put together from suggestions made by faculty in several North American, Australian and British universities and are contained in Box 7.7. One idea that is increasingly used in many subjects and areas in those parts of the world is using poster assessments (and in some subjects at large international conferences, the vast majority of presentations of research results are by poster). Details are in box 7.8(p. 124).

Principle 6: Listen

In Chapter 4 we described several ways of getting a good idea of what students are really learning. With large groups and reduced interaction with individual students it can be easy for the teacher to become cut off and short of awareness of how the course is going. We suggest that after only two or three weeks of classes you ask students some questions about how they feel the class is going. Pass around some slips of paper and ask students to write one thing they like and one thing they don't like about the class. The slips should be unsigned and collected by a student. At the next class respond to their points, and thank them for the compliments received. Repeat this; it shouldn't be a onetime exercise.

Course evaluations should also be good sources of information for improving things next year. That is likely to be true if you can design your own evaluation form or, better still, evaluate the course by pyramiding groups of students who are told to suggest the best ways to improve the course next time around. When you have to use a standard form the quality of information you get is likely to be poor with there being an excellent chance that the questions will not fit your teaching methods.

While it's important to listen, it has also to be accepted that some students

7.7. Eight Hints For Reducing The Assessment Load.

1. Search for alternatives to long-answer questions. Typically, these are problems that demand the application of knowledge, where the student has to suggest a solution, or identify key features or principles in a restricted space (say, 200 words). The words are a taut representation of complex thinking. Again, set a short essay instead of a long one. A 1000-word answer requires students to show thinking, rather than to engage in extensive description, and in the process they have to learn the discipline of concision.

2. Explore the possibility of grading presentations made in small group situations. Boxes 4.8 and 6.3 contain suggested procedures.

3. Have groups of students, rather than individual students submit papers.

4. Use assessment criteria and keywords when grading tests that cannot be objectively graded. Once you and the students are familiar with them (a) you should be able to mark quicker, and (b) the students should be producing work that is more "on target," hence easier to grade.

5. Get students to complete self-assessment sheets on which they rate their work according to the rubric or criteria, which should be printed on the sheet. This is good for students, in that it forces them to think about the criteria and encourages a reflective cast of mind. It also allows you to mark more quickly because you can give a lot of feedback by simply responding to students' self-assessments: Peter's feedback is often, "I agree. Spot-on!"

6. Do you need to mark and grade *all* parts of an assignment or test? For example, a math lecturer sets ten problems a week. All are marked in class, as he works through the solutions. He then takes in the papers and checks the grading and/or remarks one question out of the ten.

7. Do a *fast* read-through, separate answers into piles and assign rough grade levels in pencil. Then read all in more detail for more specific grade.

8. Prepare a sheet with criteria on, and make comments below each criterion, to save repeating: a yes/no check off is possible and the sum of checks gives the mark.

will not be happy, even though feedback from students regarding this active learning approach to large classes is generally very positive. Approximately 5% to 15% of the students in any one course dislike this kind of treatment, often complaining that they just want to sit and listen to an expert, not have to work with other students who know less than they. We might speculate that students who have done very well in lecture courses might be reluctant to see a change of teaching style that might see them receive lower grades. We might also speculate that some of the discontented students might simply be lazy, preferring to cruise through a lecture rather than work in a class meeting.

To rebalance things: here are a number of comments collected about the poster sessions within large geography classes:

7.8. Assessing Posters.

Groups for Posters should not exceed four students. If you have as many as 100 groups, you would need at least four poster sessions for evaluation. You will find that 25 is as many as the average faculty member can evaluate in an hour or so, although the posters can be collected for later review. Due dates should be strictly enforced

Students should be allowed to choose their own topics, though, subject to the approval of the teacher, and to advice on the range of topics to be considered. They should, as ever, have a copy of the rubric to be used in the assessment of the poster. This one is used in an introductory Geography course at the University of Lethbridge

A   An excellent poster which adheres to all the technical requirements regarding size, content and presentation and is generally attractively presented. You might wish to use + or - to indicate your degree of certainty or to reward a poster which is particularly innovative or attractive, humorous or well presented and supported by the response of the presenters to questions.

B   A good poster that adheres to most of the technical requirements but not all, yet is well-presented and supported, interesting, humorous or attractive. Alternatively you might wish to describe with a B a poster which is all technically present but is poorly or carelessly (spelling!) presented, or simply dull. Again use + or - to indicate your degree of confidence or to recognize special qualities or deficiencies present.

C   A satisfactory poster with some deficiencies in technical presentation and only moderately interesting. Lack of color or inappropriate size of items such as tiny maps might be identified as reasons for only moderate interest generated. Indifferent response to questions might cause you to add a - while good response might cause you to add a +.

D   An unsatisfactory poster which has many technical deficiencies or misrepresents the topic or is rather dull. Again, use + or - to designate your confidence in this assessment.

F   No poster or a poster which is hopelessly in conflict with the technical requirements or is deadly dull or completely wrong in some of its facts or representations. No + or - is needed here.

Reduce the marking time further by giving students a list of six to ten posters they must each mark—it also encourages them to learn from each other's posters. Half of the class display their posters while the other half, and the teacher, evaluate them. Since each poster will be graded by at least 24 students, you can be quite confident about the reliability of the mean of the peer-assessed mark for each group's poster. Techniques were described in Box 6.3 for getting individual marks from group marks.

"Poster Sessions are more fun … because you're interested in it and it doesn't seem like work."

"You learn better in a group because everybody discusses things and you help each other to learn."

"You teach each other."

"Posters give you the incentive to go out and learn on your own -- you learn because you want to learn."

"When you do it yourself you remember it -- not when you're just told."

"Better than an essay— more of an interactive way of learning."

"When you write a (research) essay you just copy down words. In a poster project you have to think and understand so that you can answer questions that people might ask."

"Posters take way more time than spitting out an essay, but you learn more."

Epilogue

The scene is a December evening on campus. Robin and Chris meet walking out to the parking lot.

Chris: Hi Robin: I hate this time of year — a pile of essays and final exams to mark, and the family is bugging me to shop before Christmas, in fact Terry wants me to take a few days off, but I can't. Too much to do. Have you already finished marking?

Robin: Yes, I now stay clear of final exams: the extra few days it gives me before Christmas I really appreciate. And why give students a message of "finality" when we all know that learning is a continuous and never-ending process? It gives me a chance to take a holiday and to get everything ready for next year before the new semester begins.

Chris: I have to thank you for teaching me so much about large classes. I even volunteered to take a large Introductory Economics class next semester: and I plan to structure it just like your class.

Robin: Wonderful! You'll enjoy it, and so will the students. Happy Christmas!

Chris: And to you Robin! Now I'm going plan to change the assessment and get a Christmas holiday next year!

8. Mainly for New Faculty, Sessional Staff, and Teaching Assistants

Preview

Departments are often, and usually unintentionally, less supportive of peripheral people (new faculty, sessional staff and teaching assistants) than we would hope. This means that it falls to you to get the help and support that are important for your development as a teacher.

You should have a mentor. If not, look for one yourself.

Network with others in similar situations to yourself.

Start and keep updating a teaching portfolio.

You will face a teaching-research conflict. While it can verge upon the insoluble, there are things you can do to make it more manageable.

Introduction

> What is key to a more orderly and enlightened [teaching] profession? Of many factors, [Ronald] Barth underscores collegiality. Collegiality means something different from congeniality, Barth emphasizes. It's just not good manners and telling jokes in the teachers' room. Collegiality means working together in a mutually supportive and thoughtful way at the business of education. Barth borrows a four-way characterization of collegiality from Judith Warren Little. In a collegial atmosphere, teachers talk about practice, observe each other, work on curriculum together, and teach each other. The school that serves as a home for teachers' minds is much more likely to become one for students' minds as well. (Perkins, 1992, p. 222)

This chapter is about people who can have a peripheral place in a departmental community and so be separated from the ideal of collegial teaching and learning discourses. Nothing here modifies our views about good teaching learning and assessment practices but we do consider what these teachers might want to do

---

in order to fine-tune themselves into a more settled professional position. Ideally, all of them would be in mentoring relationships, and that is one theme of this chapter. We hasten to add, though, that mentoring is in our view no substitute for a good collegial working environment. The routine expectations and practices of a community of practice will have more impact on new members' behavior than any mentoring scheme can ever have. The second theme of this chapter is that each of these groups of teachers should be thinking about keeping a teaching portfolio. We explain why and offer advice about it.

Table 8.1 illustrates the relationship of these twin themes of mentoring and portfolios with the peripheral standing of the three groups at the heart of this chapter.

Table 8.1
Peripheral People and Teaching in Higher Education

Peripheral Group	Key Issues	Mentoring Needs	Portfolio Purpose
New, tenure-track faculty	Coping with teaching when research is a priority. Teaching and marking efficiently. Getting somewhat above average teaching evaluations.	A colleague who understands how the tenure system *really* works. A colleague to advise on how not to kill yourself teaching.	Demonstrate teaching competence (not excellence–that can even be counter-productive) for tenure committee.
Sessional staff and part-timers	Learning departmental expectations. Having teaching excellence recognized. Getting good student evaluations. Doing it efficiently.	A mentor! None provided for most sessional staff. They concentrate on ways of building a teaching reputation.	Demonstrate teaching excellence when looking for other jobs or for a tenure-track post.
Teaching assistants	Learning how to teach and mark work. Learning how to teach and mark efficiently.	Placement in a GTA teaching program is the first priority. Scheduled teaching reviews with the professor whose class you're taking.	Demonstrate teaching excellence when looking for post-doctoral jobs.

One final introductory point. Mentoring and keeping portfolios might be urgent concerns for peripheral people but both have considerable potential for established faculty, especially—even mainly—where they are used within a continuing and formative process of personal and professional development. Consequently, much that follows could also be read to apply to established teachers who are aiming to fine tune their teaching practices. And, it goes without saying that Chairs and Heads of Departments who are interested in teaching improvement will want to think about portfolios and mentoring as departmental objects of desire.

Using Mentors

It is important that these new teachers and researchers are well guided in their early years. For example, Boice argues that

> ...the first years for new faculty are formative and lasting ... early experiences in the classroom ... and in other academic activities, such as publishing ..., predict more about career habits than any other formative period ... Once under way, career paths might be hard to change. (1992, p. 40)

The research literature is consistent in saying that new academics welcome the freedom they have in their jobs and are also often worried by it, feeling isolated and uncertain about what they should be doing. Their work environments are friendly, but not so collegial as they might have wished, leaving them to find their own solutions in the complex worlds they had entered. In particular, they have to find a balance between teaching, service, and research, although senior colleagues' expectations were not often made clear. This can be much harder for sessional staff and TAs, whose standing is far more ambiguous. Overall, new faculty's workloads are heavy, but not unsupportable. For sessional, staff, and TAs the workload that comes from teaching (perhaps for several colleges), researching and family commitments can be crushing, something that is not always well recognized. Although new faculty usually say that they enjoy the work, a number always says that the job was only possible because they have no family responsibilities and others say that there is a tension between home and work.

Accounts of new faculty members' teaching experiences show that there are problems there, which we illustrate with quotations from a study that Peter did.

> "I don't think that in terms of teaching I got any help—no that's not right, I got some notes from someone who taught the course before, I got some assignments."

> "... you were just given the course title and that was it!"

> ... so teaching at the moment is much more of a strain in this job

than has been previously. The demands are higher, and the student dissatisfaction greater. There's much more of a sense that they are "paying" for their education and they want it delivered as a consumable item in a very neat package … I'm becoming less committed to [teaching] in a sense that it doesn't pay the dividends that it should. It's getting away from my research.

Mentoring arrangements should have helped with teaching problems but although Peter heard about good arrangements for the first day in the new job, there were enough bad stories to cause unease ("We wandered around wondering what we were supposed to do. We found that these rooms were our offices. We went and sat in them but we didn't know what to do".) When it came to formal induction sessions and courses, some new faculty members found them hard to schedule, too general, or too intimidating, although there was a minority view that these activities "are very, very useful … and have changed my way of teaching and delivering lectures."

The biggest objection to orientation sessions and courses was that they did not fit with what these new hires needed to learn and do in their specific situations. So, "I didn't go [to that induction session] but that's... because I'll ask next door….In actual fact the most effective way of helping me to get into things is just informal." The disadvantage was that learning on the job could be a demanding self-help activity. Clearly, some of these new postholders had, in effect, to induct themselves, while others had found friendly colleagues who were doing some of the things that a mentor might have done. That turns attention to the operation of the mentoring arrangements.

The implications for TAs, sessional staff, and new faculty are (a) look for and take advantage of any university-wide induction program or other instructional development opportunities, and (b) look for a buddy in the department, someone who is a ready source of advice. In some ways the second of these points amounts to advising you to find a mentor.

In the original story of Mentor and Telemakhos, his protégé, Mentor acts as guide or wise counsel, a promoter who urges appropriate action and a companion in the initial path chosen. He allows independence of thought and action and remains a lifelong supporter of his protégé. There has been substantial interest in using such a relationship in universities, and not just because of the potential benefits for the protégé. One of the most interesting aspects of mentoring is that the relationship might have a profound effect on the mentor, who has to become explicit and reflective about practices that might have been routinized and implicit. The mentor might also learn directly from the protégé. This might be sufficient encouragement for established faculty to take on the role of mentoring: it can be a great way to revive your own flagging enthusiasm for teaching.

Desirable though some mentoring arrangements are as adjuncts to well-run departments, not all new faculty have mentors, as the following exchange shows, and fewer sessional staff and TAs have them.

Interviewer: So, there is no formal arrangement for helping you to enter the job?

Respondent: No ...

Interviewer: Is there anyone in the Department who has the position of being your mentor or guide?

Respondent: I don't think so. I know the Chair here in Physics, he is very helpful.... Like I expected, basically, zero help. But he told me there might be by some funds, so he's helping, trying to remind me to do things.

Even in sophisticated systems there can be surprising gaps in mentoring provision:

> "Well, we're given an administration mentor and research mentor: not a teaching one, interestingly."

For new academics and other peripheral people the research does tend to suggest that you get the quality of support and advice, from formal mentoring and informal "buddy system" mentoring, that you seek and create.

> But there is no real induction in terms of how to do the job, that's all informal and has come through in the various discussions I've had with the people I interact with the most closely....[But] it is incoherent because those people don't liaise with each other so you have to create the coherence and piece all of this together....There's lots of little micro-politics happening here because of people's own agendas. One person will encourage you to do one thing and another will get you to do something else because of theirs.... and it's also part of the induction process of learning what the micro-politics are....That's something no one really tells you about but it's part of the assimilation process, the way the academic world is; the forward agenda and the hidden agendas.

Box 8.1 draws together the research to offer some advice on mentoring relationships for peripheral people and Box 8.2 offers Administrators a summary of the features of good mentoring systems.

8.1 Good Mentoring Relationships

These points relate principally to formal mentoring arrangements. Bear in mind that formal mentors might be expected to make a summative judgment about your development, which can stunt their role as advisors who need to know your problems and difficulties if they are to give good advice.

- The earlier mentoring starts, the better.
- Formal mentoring should continue for at least several months of regular interactions, by which time you should feel bonded and the relationship should be self-sustaining.
- Make sure that regular meetings are scheduled with your mentor. Treat it as your job, not theirs.
- Mentoring cannot fix problems that are rooted in the ways that people in a department work and interact: it cannot fix misuses of power, change hierarchies or end indifference to unfairness. There will be a great deal that you will not learn in your mentoring relationship.
- You need to have a say in who mentors you. If a formal mentor is appointed who is not to your taste, then consider finding yourself an informal mentor. There is disagreement about whether it is best to have a mentor from outside your department or not. There is some evidence that an outside perspective is useful, not least because things that might otherwise be taken for granted get examined. On the other hand, someone in the department knows how it operates.
- Expect to set a lot of the agenda. The relationship will depend upon you far more than on the mentor. Never think of yourself as "being mentored." Think of yourself "using a mentor," "interacting with an experienced colleague," or "consulting with a mentor."
- Get the mentor to help, from the beginning, on the development of your teaching portfolio. Portfolios might be new to them (tenured faculty seldom keep them) but they can be useful people to talk with about what the portfolio might get to look like.

Mentors are wise but they will have points of view that are distinctive. That is valuable *and* there are other points of view and other agenda. In some universities, it is common to collect more than one mentor.

8.2. Good Mentoring Systems

Milton Cox, who has 18 years experience of running a mentoring program for new academic staff in Ohio, offers advice "on designing or continuing a mentoring program for junior faculty" (1997, p. 248). He advocates

- a carefully-designed, campus-wide program of mentoring and professional support.
- careful identification of prospective mentors.
- that persons mentored should select mentors from a university-wide list of those willing to do the job.
- a menu of activities for regular meetings (and the program coordinator should prompt mentors and mentored to make sure that meetings are regular).
- that the mentoring program should be managed by a professional program coordinator.

Research by Robert Boice stresses:

- That mentoring must be planned and systematic. Informal mentoring reaches only a third of new teachers and "the single biggest advantage of natural mentoring goes almost exclusively to white males already in the old-boy network" (Boyle & Boice, 1998, p. 159).
- Mentoring structures need to be carefully designed, for example, "provide incentives for pairs to meet" (p. 174).
- Induction and mentoring need to be fully planned and resourced on a university-wide basis, which includes agreeing on target program outcomes.
- Mentoring programs should be evaluated; this includes identifying exemplary mentors who could serve as models for future mentoring programs.

Networks

There is, of course, more to being successful as a teacher who is not a tenured member of faculty than being in a good mentoring relationship. Just as it is important to try to create networks with other teachers in your department, it is also important to network with people doing similar jobs in other departments. It has to be said that this might not be easy because there might be no existing networks into which you can slot. On the other hand, many universities and colleges do run teaching and learning development classes which, whatever their direct use, do bring you into contact with some people likely to be in a similar position to yours. Classes for TAs are also common and even if you are experienced as a TA (or as a part-time teacher) it is worth joining a class as a way of making links with others. Alternately, you might need to create your own networks. Box 8.3 lists some of the reasons why networking is valuable and Box 8.4 lists a few ways of creating or entering into a community of interest.

As with mentors, the bottom line has to be that it is up to you to find or make networks to support you in your peripheral position. And, as with mentoring, one of the main ways in which networks make a difference is that they prompt you to think about what you do, why and with what demonstrable effects. In other words, they encourage you to be a reflective practitioner. If you want to progress to a more secure status then you will normally need to show that you are skilled as a teacher, which will usually involve showing that your practices are sound (which typically means that you have good student evaluation scores) and that they are based on something more than a whim (which is usually means that you have to demonstrate that you are a reflective practitioner).

Good evaluation scores will tend to come from following the fine-tuning suggestions we have made in earlier chapters. Claiming to be a reflective practitioner means producing a teaching portfolio (or dossier, profile or record of achievement, according to local terminology).

8.3. Potential Benefits of Networking for Peripheral People

- *Reassurance.* You are not the only one in this position. Other people are in it or have been in it.
- *Support.* Isolation is a common feeling in academic life. Networks frequently provide a lot of emotional support and help you to see that failings might not be as great nor as unusual as you imagine, as well as suggesting that the source of problems is not your personal deficiencies but the conditions under which you are expected to work. Perhaps the most important thing that networks do is to let many people see that they are doing honorable things in impossible situations.
- *Advice.* People who have been through the problems that peripheral people face can offer advice on coping strategies and on longer-term planning.
- *Materials and techniques.* Often colleagues will say something on the lines of "here's a copy of what I do. Why don't you fit it to your course?" or describe ways in which they cut down on the marking load for their sophomore year course.
- *Space.* Time talking to colleagues, whether socially or professionally, is time in which you have a bit more space (peripheral people often feel uneasy about taking time out from the word-processor and the web) and can reflect on things from an easier and more spacious vantage point.
- *Efficiency.* Together you can work on common issues that could never have been tackled alone or as well. A good shared activity is to work together on improving your teaching portfolios.

8.4. Networking for Learning and Teaching

- Approach your professional development (faculty development, instructional development) office and explore the possibility of them sponsoring brown bag lunches for TAs, sessional staff, or new faculty members. You might want to insist that the spirit should be very much that of a lunch group where people with a common interest meet socially and to hear and talk about matters of common interest.
- Explore with your staff association or postgraduate association the possibilities for similar brown bag lunches under their sponsorship.
- Some groups tend to be systematically disadvantaged in higher education—women, Latinos, the disabled, for example. You might want to piggyback a teaching and learning network on one of these existing networks. In Canada the Chilly Climate Collective is a network of faculty concerned by discrimination against women in academic life.
- Subject associations often have networks dedicated to teaching and learning. Local meetings might be feasible, especially in bigger conurbations.
- Go it alone: One friend decided that creativity was under threat in her institution and convened a half-day seminar, *Creativity Under Pressure.* A couple of colleagues introduced the problem, as they saw it, and outlined some ways of approaching it. Discussions led to action plans and the formation of a network that continues to support those who want a more creative approach to learning and teaching in the university.
- Go it alone on the Internet. There are advantages to trying to get electronic exchanges between people on the same site but there is also a great deal to be had from joining in the POD or AAHE networks, or in the UK, SEDA and the National Postgraduate Committee.

Teaching Portfolios

The Dalhousie University Office of Instructional Development and Technology (OIDT) has sponsored an annual "Recording Teaching Accomplishment Institute" since 1995. The week-long international event provides faculty with the opportunity to work intensively on their portfolios in a supportive atmosphere, an atmosphere in which collegiality reigns. The following comments, submitted by participants in the 1995, 1996 and 1997 Institutes, attest that portfolios prompt reflection:

> "The process was extremely helpful in forcing me to look behind my past activities to the underlying principles which shaped them, as well as attempting to clarify what future I want to have."

> "It was a very satisfying process. It made me think about who I really was as a teacher. It is good to 'know' oneself. Developing this dossier was very rewarding."

> "Compiling my dossier has provided me with 'time-out' to reflect on the past, present and future of my university teaching career. I am very satisfied with the process, albeit tedious and humbling at times."

We have already touched upon teaching portfolios (see Table 1.2). What they, profiles, dossiers, and records of achievement have in common is that they are purposeful collections of evidence of achievement, generally with reflective commentary which explains what achievement is being shown by which piece of evidence. Consequently, portfolios can include a range of writing, of photographs, testimonials and any other items that can be interpreted as evidence of achievement. They are not mere collections. The most important part is the commentary that precedes the evidence and that makes the claim that you are a good and reflective practitioner. Confusingly, some people describe this introductory piece, which might be about eight pages long, as the teaching dossier. Here, when we talk about a portfolio, we are referring to the claim to be reflective *and* to the archive of accompanying evidence.

The main message of this section is to start one. Tenured faculty can get away with studied indifference to many things. In contrast, peripheral people continually need to be able to give an account of their achievements and the teaching portfolio is the recognized way of doing it.

Portfolios can have high stakes uses, as when you use a portfolio in a tenure case, or low stakes, when they are used to identify areas for your own development. Formative (low stakes) portfolios are likely to be more open than summative (high stakes) portfolios, since the latter, intended to show achievement alone encourage the creators of the portfolio to aim to put the best gloss on their achievements—a gloss that might be a deceptive one. Formative dossiers, intended to be a basis for planning for development, are less likely to be exercises in image management and should disclose more and be more open. A third sort of portfolio has an ipsative purpose, which is to say that the intention is to show changes in a person's current achievement as compared to his/her past attainment. These will mainly be for personal use, as prompts to reflection and as celebrations of progress.

Table 8.2 summarizes claims that have been made about the strengths and weaknesses of teaching portfolios. Boxes 8.5 through 8.7 advise on making a portfolio.

Table 8.2.
Claimed Strengths of and Problems with Teaching Portfolios

Strengths	Problems
Provide a tool for reflection on teaching.	Resistance, especially from tenured, mid-career faculty
Improves teaching performance	Burdensome
Provides information for teaching awards	Marginalized by low status of teaching compared to research
Maintain a record of teaching accomplishments	Incompatible with higher education systems facing intensification and overload
Provide a context for career planning	Difficult to assess
Are a source of information for present and prospective employers	Difficult to introduce universally with success
Support mentoring	Promotion, tenure, and review committees might fail to give proper weight to portfolios
Encourage the establishment of effective criteria for teaching	
Encourage esteem for teaching, giving it attention and a voice	
Provide a better basis for dialogue on teaching	

8.5 A Ten-step Portfolio Creation Program

1. Start a "dump file" now. Routinely throw into a box (electronic or otherwise) anything that could be used to show that you are a good teacher.
2. Be clear what your teaching responsibilities are.
3. Work out what criteria are tacitly applied to judging teaching quality in your department or academic unit. You can then either pitch your dossier in terms of those criteria, do that and add others, or put forward criteria taken from another authoritative source and hang your portfolio around them.
4. Describe your approach to teaching, including your goals and philosophy (and why it is good for students, the department and the university).
5. If you have not already done so, make your claims to be a good teacher: what are the grounds you have for claiming strength as a teacher?
6. Select material for the dossier (see Box 8.6 on the most often used material). The material will evidence that your claims to strength can be taken seriously.
7. Cross tabulate your claims with the material, preparing a statement for each claim that refers to the material and explains why any one item is good evidence for a particular claim.
8. Further order the material. There might be several items supporting one claim. It might make sense to arrange them chronologically to show a development in your performance on this claim.
9. Keep copies!
10. Revise your *curriculum vitae* so that it refers at some length to your portfolio. You might wish to tune early parts of your portfolio to fit with the CV. The two documents go together.

(This draws upon the work of Carol O'Neil and Alan Wright, 1995.)

Administrators should encourage sessional staff, TAs, and new faculty to develop portfolios.

First of all, teaching portfolios must be valued. University teachers must see that the writing of the teaching portfolio is a worthwhile enterprise in its own right. They must be convinced that the expenditure of time and resources is worthwhile and that they will learn from the experience. That message needs to come from Chairs, Heads of Departments and other senior colleagues, and to appear in induction and orientation courses, as well as in mentoring programs. In what way does a departmental or institutional culture demonstrate that it values effective teaching? There are many ways. A Biology Department Head hands a copy of his own teaching portfolio to a newly-hired assistant professor, literally delivering the message that teaching is recognized as important in the Department and that the portfolio is an appropriate way of signaling the emphasis on teaching. A Humanities Department announces an opening for a tenure track position. Both teaching and research capabilities are emphasized in the published advertisement. The Department requires applicants to submit a teaching dossier and short-listed candidates to deliver a guest presentation. Finally, teaching portfolios become a standard part of the nomination files for campus teaching awards.

For the teaching portfolio to take root, teaching must be rewarded in the institutional setting and it must be seen to be rewarded. In the university environment, this means that in the renewal, tenure, and promotion process teaching must be on a level playing field with research. It means that tenure and promotion committees must give teaching portfolios serious attention. They must clearly indicate that they are reversing two related tendencies which have plagued the process in many institutions in the past: that of considering teaching only as a "pass-fail" aspect of a faculty member's file rather than examining teaching in a more nuanced fashion on a scale equivalent to the one employed for research; and that of considering teaching only as a significant component of performance when it is done particularly poorly! For portfolios to become truly embedded in the university culture, candidates must know that their submitted teaching records will get more than summary treatment and that the positive evidence contained in a teaching portfolio can lead to tangible rewards.

The assumption so far has been that teaching improvement is something that peripheral people feel that it is important to concentrate upon. That is a little naive, since research productivity has become the prime performance indicator in higher education in the English-speaking world. That research-teaching dilemma is the topic of the next section.

Box 8.7. Teaching Portfolio Do's and Don'ts

Do:
- Open a dump file now.
- Review the dump file periodically and then update the portfolio; make a note in your calendar to remind you.
- Involve others in reviewing your portfolio. This means use the networks you are in, mentors and other staff in the department. Value highly the comments of colleagues in other departments or universities.
- Ask others (a) what do you think my main claims are, and (b) on the basis of what you've read, do you believe them?
- Do an ICT check. Is your portfolio looking a bit dated because you say nothing about ICT in your teaching?
- Do an employability check. Is your portfolio looking a bit dated because it says nothing about the ways in which your teaching encourages the development of general skills and qualities that are valued in the employment and postgraduate markets?
- Act on ideas that strike you when you revise your portfolio: revising it should give you ideas about doing some more fine-tuning to your teaching. That becomes material for the next revision.

Don't:
- Heap material into the portfolio; give a few examples of each claim and note other evidence that you can produce if asked.
- Put material in the portfolio without numbering it. Then use cross references to those numbers in your opening statements, where you explain what each item is supposed to be demonstrating.
- Be modest.
- Treat it as a private activity. Reflection works best when there are others to reflect off and with.

(This draws upon the work of Carol O'Neil and Alan Wright, 1995.)

The Teaching-Research Dilemma and Peripheral People

Seldin and associates (1990) state, as we noticed in Chapter 1, that teaching is widely undervalued in the university environment and say, as do many, many other commentators, that,

> The approach seems to be to talk about the importance of teaching, but to evaluate faculty primarily on the basis of scholarly achievements and professional activities. . . . The faculty member more interested in teaching than in scholarly research is soon forced by the institution's reward system to "go with the program." (pp. 3, 4)

TAs want to get to be tenure track faculty, which means publishing; sessional staff who want to get more secure status will also usually have to have a good publication record, and new faculty will need a good research profile to make it past committees who know it is cheaper to staff a department with hopefuls and part-timers than it is to give tenure. So, how to be good at research *and* at teaching? One observation is that most subjects and areas have journals that publish scholarly papers on the teaching of the subject. In this sense, being a better teacher can lead to publication and there is no tension between teaching and research.

A more extensive answer holds that the solution is not entirely about being more efficient as teachers. Box 8.8 contains a set of timesaving suggestions for teachers, which is our modest contribution to reducing the work overload on faculty. But in many cases overload is not up to the teaching load. Two obvious sources of time problems are:

8.8. Time-savers for Teachers (see also Box 7.7 on Assessment Time-savers)

Test Construction: It takes considerable time and effort to develop MCT questions that allow you to make a valid and reliable inference. One way of generating them is to require students to write a dozen (with answers), try them out on each other and then submit them for your assessment. There are excellent software packages, e.g., LXRTest out now that help you automatically bank your test questions for use in tests down the road. See also Nitko (1996).

Grade Sheets: Use LXRTest or similar software packages to help you keep track of your marks. If not, use a regular spreadsheet. The spreadsheet can keep students apprised of their current marks and converted grades. Once you have programmed it, it can be used year after year. All you need to do is make the slight adjustments necessary—for example change the demographic data, perhaps change a weighting on an assignment or test here and there, but that's all.

Remembering Names of Students: Students appreciate your attempts to remember their names, and it makes for a smoother running and more efficient class if you do. A good way to solve this is by taking their photos with a digital camera on the first day of class. First have the students make name tags out of 11 x 8 sheets of paper folded in half lengthwise, then have each row line up with their name tags at chest level and then take the photo. Download them into your computer. Be sure to get student permission first because of such Acts as the Freedom of Information and Privacy (FOIP).

Housekeeping: This time-saver is a general one and can be applied in a variety of circumstances. Have the students do the housekeeping tasks in your class, such as handing out papers, turning off lights for video projections, recording notes on the overhead projector while you can focus the class discussion and not have to record simultaneously, run the video cassette recorder, and other such equipment.

Less Teaching for More Learning: Do you need to be with a class so often? Consider this English example. A course that traditionally had 40 staff-student contact hours was recognized

---

as one that involved 270 student learning hours. A design to make the best use of that learning time ended up with 32 staff-student contact hours. This gave some easement to the faculty member teaching the course, making the management of a large class easier. A parallel redesign of the assessment requirements (substitution of a presentation for an essay and the production of an annotated, ten item reading lists for another) had a similar effect.

Giving Feedback: If students did pre-submission appraisals of their own or each other's work, they would pick up points on which you would not then need to comment

Office Hours: A lot of time can be saved if individuals can only see you for consultations at set times of your choosing. Get a rule that everything else is dealt with by E-mail.

Redirecting Inquiries: The second person who asks an E-mail question gets the answer you gave the first person (and which you saved). When someone is not sure of a technique or procedure, first ask them if their Action Learning Set can help and then, second, put them onto a student who you have already told how to do it. That will help both students, the "teacher" and the learner. A listserve set up early in the semester will do the same thing; here you can add things that you want them to bring to next class that you forgot to mention, or send out reminders for them, etc.

Group Consultations: Aim to give advice to groups, not to individuals. That means that you should reduce the scope for individuals to negotiate their own assignment themes or topics. Here is a case when time saving needs to be weighed against the educational case for choice and diversity.

Seniors Teach Freshmen: On some courses it makes sense for seniors to do some Freshman year teaching. Not to be used indiscriminately.

Plagiarism: If you set the same assignments year on year, then the chances of plagiarism are high and this is likely to tie up a lot of your time in trying to detect it. Questions 11 and 12 in Chapter 9 contain good advice for saving time by reducing the room for plagiarism.

Poor time management in general. Many people have lousy time management methods. That is not to say that time management courses can solve all of the problems, because often habits that look like they are wasting time serve other important personal and psychological functions. Nevertheless, many people would benefit from having a one touch approach to paper and to E-mails (see it and do it unless it really does want sustained reflection); from setting priorities and making more use of the trash can than of the file cabinet; from working in shorter and focused spells; and so on—any time management course is replete with ideas like these.

Poor research practices. If the concept of fitness for purpose were more prominent in research practices, then a lot of time would be saved. Given a study's purpose and audience, it is often the case that a research design can be streamlined. Why are interviews routinely transcribed? Why are so many questions asked? How many people need to see and revise a draft report? One of the biggest blocks to research efficiency is people's writing practices. Boice (1992) found that those new hires who put off writing up their research until they had clear blocks of writing time were far less productive (and more stressed) than those who wrote a little on most days. Adopting sound writing habits enhances productivity and makes for greater career success. An examination of what happens in the black box labeled "Research" can show some very inefficient practices.

Disclaimer

It can be very stressful to be on the edges of a community of established and successful-looking academics. How stressful it feels is somewhat down to you. For sure, there are departments which are friendly, considerate and with good induction and mentoring systems in place. There are many that are unthinkingly indifferent to you. A theme of this chapter is that it is necessary for you to make the difference: to be proactive in mentoring, to look out or create networks; to get a teaching portfolio up and going; and to question the ways in which you allocate time and see whether it is habits rather than external demands that make a workload seem to be unbearable.

It is not a position with which we are happy because it comes very close to blaming the victims for their plight and to blaming peripheral people for being on the edges. We are not saying that we approve of the changes in teaching arrangements that have meant that in some universities Freshmen do not meet tenured professors and that the quality of teaching is better in many community colleges than it is in the first two years of many university programs. But that is the way things are and the signs are that casualization of the academic professions is not yet done (and compared to the USA it is hardly started in Britain).

Our suggestions for new faculty, sessional staff, and TAs have been designed to help individuals in situations that are far from ideal.

9: Frequently Asked Questions

Concerns people have about teaching are far more diverse than we have been able to capture in the preceding chapters. Our strategies for fine-tuning teaching practices are powerful ones but they run the risk of ignoring the specific glitches, the bugs in the system, and the seemingly-impossible dilemmas that do so much to make our practices discordant with our intentions. This chapter acknowledges that our teaching could be fine-tuned if we could get around specific problems whose impact is disproportionate to their apparent size.

We have presented a selection of problem-shooting ideas in the form of a newspaper or magazine advice column. Running through our suggestions are the twin themes that most problems have a solution and that you might like the solution a good deal less than the problem.

1. And I've My Career to Think Of!

Dear Nola,

I have a mentor in the department I joined last year. He's a great guy and very well respected for his research in Psychology. The problem is that his advice is contrary to everything I read in books like yours: he recommends short course outlines that commit the teacher to as little as possible, a single midterm test, a major final exam. He also says I should spend no more than 50 minutes in preparing a 50-minute lecture. Otherwise, he says, my research will suffer. Now, that sure makes sense to me but I do know that the tenure committee will want to see my teaching portfolio, so should I completely believe him or should I try to get a mentor who is a bit less vehement about research?

Perplexed protégé

Dear Perplexed Protégé,

Well, he's right about one thing—don't let your research suffer—but that doesn't mean let your teaching suffer either. There's something about this problem in Chapter 8, which might be a good place to go to.

In a way, though, I think you're already on the case. You're doing what mentees (yes, it's a vile word) need to do, which is taking some responsibility for your own development. Now, what you're getting obviously is not the mentoring you need for your teaching. I think you should think about finding how to get a teaching mentor. If this is done tactfully, you will be better off than getting frustrated trying to follow something that is contrary to your understanding about how people learn.

And although I know where your mentor is coming from with this research emphasis, I do get worried by people who make research into something all-consuming. I worry about the balance in their lives and, more usefully, I wonder if they're working harder when they really ought to be working smarter. But that's another theme of Chapter 8's treatment of the research-teaching dilemma.

2. Who Cares?

Dear Nola,

I just don't get it. Who cares if my teaching is being "fine-tuned"? Around here it's your research that counts. So, why bother?

Cynical,
Charlottesville, VA.

Dear Cynical,

Yes, for many tenured faculty in many institutions teaching comes at the back of the pack. This has got worse as colleges that once had teaching as their main mission have caught a dose of "publish or perish" over the past 15 years. So, in personal terms alone, it might make a lot of sense for you to put research and committee work first. The answer to the question 3 (below) says more but here I want to add that whatever the calculation of self interest says, you should *care.*

In the long run higher education depends upon three groups: students, employers and governments. Although employers sometimes benefit from some research and government occasionally does, they, like students and their tuition-paying parents, see colleges as teaching institutions. Now, if it looks as though the teaching is pretty indifferent, then you might get:

- *Students increasingly signing up with web universities that have big names behind them, well-designed on-line courses, flexible learning arrangements, and lower tuition costs. The spectacular success of Britain's Open University as a distance learning provider is a warning to colleges that think that they can deliver poor teaching combined with tuition hikes.*
- *Employers want graduates with intellectual and other qualities. If colleges don't produce them then, first, they will publicly criticize higher education, which is*

hardly in our interests, and secondly, they will increasingly run their own "universities."

- *Governments underwrite a smaller or larger proportion of the costs of higher education. Even in the free market USA, funding from government sources of one sort and another is very significant. Those moneys are, as the assessment movement amongst state governments has shown, closely related to perceptions that colleges are doing a good job of teaching.*
- *Most importantly for us is the final point. You've taken their money with the promise of providing students with a good education. There is a lot of agreement as to what that looks like. So do it. It's a moral matter.*

3. Looking Good

Dear Nola,

I want my teaching to look good to accrediting agencies and other observers but I don't want to spend too long on it. Any ideas?

Meretricious,
Manchester, UK

Dear Meretricious,

One of my colleagues said that I should put this in the trash and not waste time on helping people play at spin doctors by varnishing the appearance and doing nothing for the substance. I think you have to start somewhere and if you start with the looks of your teaching, then it might prove to be infectious. My ten tips are these:

1. *Get a handful of learning outcomes – choose from all four columns in Table 1.1.*
2. *Update your course syllabus document or course handbook. Good documentation always impresses onlookers.*
3. *Make sure the handbook refers to ICT and, preferably, that there is at least one assignment that has students using the web to get information or to discuss a topic.*
4. *Use video clips, slides, or ICT-based materials in some of your presentations. Flag it up prominently in the handbook.*
5. *Make sure that OHTs look good. Use Corel Presentation, Microsoft PowerPoint© or a word processor (which is usually more flexible than PowerPoint©).*
6. *Spend some time (sorry, this is not quite a no-effort answer) on the way you*

look and sound as a lecturer/presenter. Voice, posture, body language, and enthusiasm are the things to go for.

7. Have some interactions in presentations: simple things like a show of hands, 30 seconds think time, three minutes share with your neighbor time.

8. As for assessment, the best but rather vague advice, is to make sure that it is as clear as possible to students what they have to do to get good marks.

9. Share the examination blueprint with students and invite them to suggest questions that you could use in the exam.

10. Do an evaluation early in the course, find out what student concerns are and tell them how you will fix them.

4. But It Takes Too Much Time!

Dear Nola,

I have started to adopt some new teaching techniques such as group discussion, frequent testing and student presentations. The problem I have is that it is taking me so much time designing tests, and managing marks that I think my performance in other areas is suffering. What can I do? Revert to a steady diet of lectures and major examinations?

Exhausted,
Edinburgh, UK

Dear Exhausted,

You need a life and here are a couple of suggestions. First, why are you designing questions and assessment during the term when you are at your busiest? Assessment tasks should be designed along with the course outline (however, some fine tuning might be needed during the course because of slight changes in the course emphasis), so that they are properly aligned to your instruction. That way you and the students will have the target to aim for (because the students will know up front what they will be graded on—again that's just fair assessment practice), and you and the students will have a much less stressful time of it. Students will know what to focus on so they won't be wasting time on less important parts of the course. That way they'll learn what's important. Sorta makes sense, doesn't it?

Next, invest the time to put your marks on a spreadsheet. Set up the software to do this before the beginning of the semester. Factor in your weightings for the tasks and set up a formula so that when the time arises, you have an instant readout of the students' marks.

Other hints for cutting the load of assessing student learning are in Chapter 4 and in Box 7.7.

As for the steady diet of lectures and examinations? If you're really concerned about student learning, I think you already know the answer to the lectures part. But you could do worse than think again about variants on examinations described in Box 4.12.

5. Better Evaluations

Dear Nola,

I have been teaching for a few years at a university that prides itself on teaching excellence. The student reports on my performance are not good despite the fact that I spend a lot of time preparing my lectures and think I am friendly and approachable. What can I do to improve the ratings I get in student evaluations without simply giving everyone an A?

Unpopular,
Utah

Dear Unpopular,

First, you say think you're friendly and approachable. It might be worth just exploring what that means — are they at the expense of a concern for student learning? With students, you need to be respected and trusted, and if you're just acting friendly and approachable for points, they can see through that. Check to see if you're authentically respectful to students, and consistently so—and with all of them. It irks students to see your being respectful to some but not the others, even if they don't deserve it themselves, sometimes. Reflect on what it means to treat students respectfully, be respectful in and out of class. If you do that first, the rest will follow.

Second, to get good course evaluations, handing out "A's" willy-nilly doesn't do it. Students do not respect this desperate behavior. They might not refuse them, but that doesn't equate popularity either if that's what you're after (by the way, that's supported by research). If you're going after popularity, start with respect—and I mean genuine respect. One way to get that is through fair assessment practice and give students the grades they deserve.

Finally, taking a lot of time preparing lectures does not necessarily equate with good teaching and learning. In fact that set a few alarm bells ringing because it reminded me of research that shows that new faculty often spend a lot of time preparing the wrong lectures. I don't mean that they're lectures on the wrong topics. I mean that the lectures are chock-full of the most detailed and up-to-date information, often at a level beyond many students. These lectures sweat the business of cramming a lot of information into their lectures (and can often present it well) but neglect the need to gear their teaching to getting students to understand. *And sometimes their barrage of information is dull, dull, and dull again.*

So, I'd have another look at Chapter 5 on presentations and then begin to introduce some interactive work, bit by bit over a couple of years, from Chapter 6.

6. So, What Do I Do about these Multiple Intelligences?

Dear Nola,

I read the occasional paper in educational research and feel intimidated by many of the things I read. For instance I read recently of many different types of intelligence and learning behaviors (eight I think it was). How on earth can this help me? I teach enormous classes in a big university: I have to package everything for the average intelligence and average behavior. Does this mean that I am likely only communicating with one-eighth of any class?

Intimidated,
Idaho

Dear Intimidated,

Yes, a lot of educational research is written by specialists and for specialists, so it's as hard to understand as any other field is to lay people. Our aim was to make this a book that worked out the implications of a lot of this material in a useful and accessible form. And, although we mentioned Gardner in Chapter 2, I guess we need to say more about some implications of his work.

He is a researcher who rejected the idea that there is one type of intelligence and suggested that we have multiple intelligences (and he began by calling them "skills"). He listed seven (and then eight) of them, freely admitting that the idea that we have multiple intelligences is far more important than finalizing the exact number of them. Nor did he ever expect that every class would engage all of the intelligences at any time. Rather, it is important for teachers to be aware of them so sensitive to the different mental strengths that we all have. By using a variety of teaching strategies, such as group work, fieldwork and practical work, presentations, projects, labs, and presentations; and by using an equally wide range of assessment methods you will do a fair job of allowing students to work in their area of strength, particularly if you give them choice in their assignments. For example, some students might prefer to respond to an assigned problem through an essay, another might prefer to use a dramatic representation, another through art or a poster. The important thing here is to have a good scoring rubric that can accommodate the different ways of representing under-

standing: to supplement the ideas in Chapter 4, consult Marzano, Pickering and McTighe (1993).

Finally, I can't for the life of me I see why you're "packaging your course" to meet the "average intelligence and behavior" (whatever they are). I can understand having presentations that make sure that everyone has got a framework in which to fit information (see Chapter 5) but after that I'd have thought that good assignments would mean that higher-achievers would be able to demonstrate superior skills of synthesis, analysis, critical thinking, problem-working and evaluation. I would also expect interactive work to provide a medium that challenged all students to work slightly beyond their unaided level of achievement (see Chapter 6).

7. Covering the Ground

Dear Nola,

I can't believe the kinds of things I overheard you saying last week. With the explosion of information in the sciences, how can we cut down on the number of lectures in a science course? Maybe our Arts and Social Science friends can, but I have to go flat-out as it is to get through the basic material students will need to know to enter second year courses in Physics. If I lost even one lecture per semester the students would suffer terribly. To be honest, I am thinking of asking the Dean to assign an extra class per week for each science course. We desperately need it.

> Physicist,
> Perth, WA.

Dear Physicist,

Yes, I sympathize. Knowledge expands exponentially and no one ever cuts anything out of the curriculum, so the teacher's job gets pretty desperate if you're trying to cover all the bases. But surely that's near impossible at best and ludicrous at worst. Howard Gardner is only one of the commentators who is concerned that the quest for coverage is a damaging one. He has argued that,

> *The greatest enemy of understanding is coverage. As long as you are determined to cover everything, you actually ensure that most kids are not going to understand ... Now, this is the most revolutionary idea in American education—because most people can't abide the notion that we might leave out one decade of American history or one formula in math or one biological system. But that's crazy because we*

now know that kids don't understand those things anyway. They for-
get them as soon as the test is over—because it hasn't been built into
their brain, engraved in it. (1993, p. 7).

If you don't accept that position, then I cannot offer any sensible response to your
problem. If you do see that we have to select a little to teach from the mass that we
would like students to learn, then the suggestions are:

First, ask yourself, what's really important for students to know now and know
twenty years hence? Your answer might well identify key principles and concepts that
can be illustrated and taught by means of any one of a large number of examples. The
examples matter less than the big, key or structural concepts that have staying power.

Secondly, the students must take some responsibility for their learning. Spoon
feeding is not the answer, and students tire of it because it lacks challenge. They should
learn in all the work they do in your subject that the teachers take responsibility for
developing an understanding of the big principles and that students have responsibil-
ity for gathering information about examples of those principles and for applying the
principles to fresh, sometimes problematic settings (which takes us back to Chapter 5).

Third, set thoughtful assignments where students have to research the informa-
tion themselves or apply ideas to problems that are really fresh and challenging and
take ownership of their outcomes while you deal with the more difficult concepts. If
you keep using Classroom Assessment Techniques and the like, you'll know what's
getting missed.

8. The Language of Assessment

Dear Nola,

I've been trying to get a handle on this business of testing and doing some
reading about it, but I'm getting even more confused. Sometimes I read "test,"
other times, "measurement," sometimes "assessment," and then "evaluation."
Would you please explain the differences among them if indeed there are any?

Confused,
Kingston ON

Dear Confused,

You're right, people do use these terms interchangeably but there are subtle dif-
ferences:

Think of "tests" as the actual measuring instruments, like thermometers and
scales. Alone, they hold no value but are one of the many possible tools that we use to
assess students' progress.

"Assessment" is any systematic basis for making inferences about characteristics of people, usually based on various sources of evidence. It is a process of collecting and organizing information or data in ways that make it possible for people to then "judge" or evaluate students' understanding or competence.

"Measurement" refers to the collection of quantitative data such as test scores or numerical ratings on essays and projects. Assessment differs from measurement because it involves inference on the basis of data.

"Evaluation" depends on values. It is the final grade or judgment made from the collected assessment data.

In summary, then, we view "test" as a form of measuring instrument, such as a quiz that is given to students; "measurement" as the actual scores or numerical ratings derived from the assessment instrument; and "assessment" as the whole process of collecting evidence and inferences to make an "evaluation" or judgment about student learning or about a course, program, teaching, and institutional quality.

9. Strict Deadlines

Dear Nola,

I have a rule that if students don't hand in their assignment by the due date they get a zero—no argument entertained. Students say this is grossly unfair. I say that that's it's unfair to the others who got theirs in on time. What's good for the goose, is good for the gander. Am I right?

Zero Tolerance

Dear Zero,

I'm not sure how you handle legitimate and exceptional circumstances, but sticking so rigidly to this rule puts you in a tricky situation.

If you average in a zero to the term mark it can have a profound effect on the final mark, depending on the weighting that you've given the zero assignment. A zero on an assignment that has a 5% weighting has little consequence, but if this is a hefty assignment, the zero could be devastating. While it is frustrating to have assignments handed in late, give yourself and students some breathing space. Two ways of handling work that is seriously late are, first, to have a sliding scale of penalties that goes up to, say, a 20-point penalty, and secondly, follow Guskey's (1996) recommendation and use the student's median score for the final grade. Whatever line you take, do make sure it is clearly set out in the course syllabus or handbook.

10. Oral Presentations

Dear Nola,

I assigned student presentations in my second-year class for the first time this semester and they were mostly very poor. I only gave 5% of the final mark for the presentation, but I wanted the students to take them seriously and put some effort in. How can I get them to take the presentations seriously in future?

> Rocky,
> Rochester, UK

Dear Rocky,

I need to know a few things first about how you set the presentations up. Did you share the purpose of the presentations with the students? Was the presentation relevant? Did the students have real choice in the presentation? Did you provide clear criteria for them to follow?

I guess that there will also have been some students who calculated that preparing a good presentation is very time consuming and that it wasn't worth the investment for a maximum of 5% of the course marks.

Next time try (a) to make sure that you are very clear about what you expect and how the presentations will be graded, (b) allocate more marks to them, (c) consider cutting one or two other pieces of assessment to give students more space to take on this more authentic task, and (d) add to the stakes by making peer assessment a part of it (see Box 6.3).

PS. Was the 5% up front or did you decide on that after you saw the disappointing presentations?

11. Cheating

Dear Nola,

I teach large sections and I'm sure that the students are running rings round me by cheating in their assignments. Is there any way I can stop this without grading them just on work done in the examination halls?

> Luxated of Lethbridge, AB

Dear Luxated,

It would be naive to believe that a student has not attempted to cheat at least once in his or her life but there are several ways that you can deter cheating on tests and assignments and many are common sense.

Let's start with tests. Think back to your own experiences when you took a test: Sitting apart from your peers was certainly one way, but constant vigilance by the examiner worked better, didn't it? Research tells us that most students are worried about being caught cheating or seemingly cheating so if you show that you treat it seriously the chances of it happening are reduced. Multiple-choice questions printed on a machine-scored card make cheating easy, so it's best to use them in halls where your vigilance will deter any attempts to get inspiration from the pattern on a neighbor's card. Open-ended questions are automatic deterrents to cheating.

As for assignments, if you repeat last year's tasks, then you are asking for sharp practice. Set new tasks or select ones from an item bank that is so large that the student who has prepared to answer all of the questions has more than met the course requirements. Alternatively, give the students a meaningful assignment that relates to them personally, so that there is no advantage to doing it with another student. Set tasks that require the application of general concepts, procedures or principles to a unique case: give students notes on a case and ask them to apply their engineering knowledge to provide a solution within certain limits. Cheating on assignments like this is almost impossible.

Another way of thinking about cheating on assignments involves accepting that students do discuss questions and work on them together. We have encouraged you to think about supporting that in the shape of Action Learning Sets. Logically, it then makes sense to give them the opportunity to do a group assignment and either all take the given mark or to have individual marks allocated by one of the formulae in Box 6.3 Students will brainstorm, work cooperatively (hangers-on are given the short shrift) and you have fewer assignments to mark. Why we pretend that collaboration does not go on and then manage to think of it as illegitimate is an intriguing question. Better to make the group work legitimate and mark them as such. And you might want to look at the next question, which is about the special case of plagiarism.

12. Plagiarism

Dear Nola,

Plagiarism is running rampant thanks to the Internet. It's supporting students' grades, all right, but I'm not sure about their learning. Their grades are skyrocketing since they can plagiarize whatever they want off the Net and take credit for it. On the one hand I want them to use what the Internet has to offer, but on the other, this downright cheating has got to stop!

Irate Irma,
Inverness, UK

Dear II,

Did you not have that very same problem with reference material in hard copy form? I don't see much difference in Internet plagiarism and reference plagiarism. To avoid plagiarism set your assignments in personalized form so that taking a general essay on Hamlet will not be acceptable. Instead, have the students reveal their knowledge by having them write about how their lives mirror in some way the life of Hamlet; or they can take the stance how it doesn't, etc. If students do crib a bit off the Net essay (and inadvertently learn it at the same time), then that's well and good, because this way they have to think (horrors!) about how to use the stolen material. And that's really the hard part, isn't it, and it's the kind of thinking you want them to do anyway instead of regurgitating facts. Open-ended assignments such as these promote higher levels of thinking. And that's not a bad thing to promote—if you think about it.

If you want to spend the time tracking down electronic plagiarists, read Detecting Internet Plagiarism *(Johnson & Ury, 1998) to find out more about checking for it and getting an updated list of such handy things as Internet term paper sites. If you require all papers to be submitted electronically, you can use dedicated software to scan suspicious ones for stylistic evidence of excessive cut-and-pasting. (This was used at Edinburgh University, UK, in 1999 to establish that up to half of the freshman computer science class had submitted work containing "startling similarities." The Principal [the President] commented that "Discussion was acceptable among students, but the transfer of program solutions was not.")*

13. Tough Midterms

Dear Nola,

Students complain about my midterm tests and I think my course evaluation suffers because most of them fail it. Of course, most pass the final exam. How can I get them to relax and not get upset about failing a test which will not have a great deal of bearing on their final mark? I like the mid term test to be a "wake-up call": I remember similar tests when I was a student and I never complained.

Tester,
Texas.

Dear Tester,

I think we can say it's a given that your evaluations will be low if your tests cut through students like Ghengis Khan, although I'm curious about how most fail the midterm but you still pass them in the final. Is that because you only pass the survivors? Because the midterm is a wake-up call that they take notice of? Or because one test is too hard and/or the other is too easy?

I would wonder what the purpose of the midterm is? And why are most students failing it? Using an exam as a weapon (which it seems to be in your case) to shape up your students is not regarded as sound pedagogical practice. There are no studies that support the use of low marks as punishments—many students regard them irrelevant or meaningless—and students resent the game that you're playing.

Also, I wonder why you have to have a wake up call for all the students? I've no doubt a minority might need some reminding that they need to take the course seriously, but there's no reason to punish the lot. If you do want a wake-up call, give the students a pop quiz—one where they are not alerted ahead of time—to let you and the students know what they do and do not understand (see assessment part 2 chapter). Used diagnostically like this and not for grades, it helps you and the students to get on track about what needs more work and what can be left aside. It can be a very efficient tool for you in teaching and a nice friendly assessment to clue the students in.

Think formative and think low stakes (Chapter 4).

14. Who Am I?

Dear Nola,

I'm concerned because I think this being a better teacher stuff might mean that I have to pretend to be someone I'm not.

Mrs. Krabappel,
Springfield.

Dear Mrs. Krabappel,

Good point and not easy to answer completely. I think the stuff on the way students quickly respond to our body language does say that they respond to who we are, and since we know that certain ways of speaking, moving and acting are more attractive than others, it follows that if we want to bring the audience on-side, then we should act: big eyes, lots of teeth, plenty of gestures, confident and full voices, upright (but not stiff) stance. So, you're right in the sense that good teaching is about acting, in some measure.

But then there is the consistent finding that what students value in a teacher are Enthusiasm, Clarity, and Interest. And the same research finds that these take many forms. One person who talks nonstop for an entire session can be interesting, even if it is a joke-free zone. Another can make evolutionary biology interesting or make the idea of "dark matter" seem clear. You could interpret these findings to mean that it is what you do that is important. The implication would be that if you take a selection of the ideas in this book and develop them in ways that suit you and your workplace, then this will mean that you are trying to be a better teacher and remain in integrity with yourself.

But one last thought. Sometimes, ideas do more than give us some good hints and make us think that perhaps we should try to change. We might have made suggestions that you, on reflection, will accept with the realization that this means some change to your existing beliefs, attitudes, or values.

References

Allee, V. (1997). *The knowledge evolution*. Boston, MA: Butterworth-Heinemann.

Angelo, T. A. & Cross, K. P. (1993). *Classroom assessment techniques: A handbook for college teachers*, San Francisco: Jossey Bass.

Aoki, T. T. (1990). *Inspiriting curriculum and pedagogy: Talks to teachers*. University of Alberta, Edmonton, AB: Curriculum Praxis.

Astin, A. W. (1997). *Four years that matter: The college experience twenty years on*, paperback edition. San Francisco: Jossey-Bass.

Balderston, F. E. (1995). *Managing today's university: Strategies for viability, change, and excellence*. San Francisco: Jossey-Bass.

Barnett, R. (1994). *The limits of competence*. Buckingham & Philadelphia: Society for Research in Higher Education and the Open University Press.

Berlak, H., Newmann, F. M., Adams, E., Archbald, D. A., Burgess, T., Raven, J., & Romberg, T. A. (1992). *Toward a new science of educational testing and assessment*. New York: SUNY.

Bess, J. L. (Ed.) (1997). *Teaching well and liking it.* Baltimore: John Hopkins University Press.

Boice, R. (1992). *The new faculty member: Supporting and fostering professional development*. San Francisco: Jossey Bass.

_____. (1996) *First-Order Principles for College Teachers : Ten Basic Ways to Improve the Teaching Process*: Bolton MA: Anker

Bott, P. A. (1996). *Testing and assessment in occupational and technical education*. Needham Heights, MA: Allyn & Bacon.

Boud, D. (1995). *Enhancing learning through self-assessment*, London: Kogan Page.

Boyle, P. & Boice, R. (1998). Systematic mentoring for new faculty teachers and graduate teaching assistants. *Innovative Higher Education, 22* (3), 157-179.

Brown, J. L. & Moffett, C. A. (1999). *The hero's journey: How educators can transform schools and improve learning*. Alexandria, VA: Association for Supervision and Curriculum Development.

Brown, S. & Knight, P. (1994) *Assessing learners in higher education*. London: Kogan Page.

Checkley, K. (1997). The first seven…and the eighth: A conversation with Howard Gardner. *Educational Leadership, 55* (1), 8-13.

Cooper, R. K. & Sawaf, A. (1997). *Executive EQ*. London: Orion Business Books.

Costa, A. L., & Kallick, B. (1992). Reassessing assessment. In A.L Costa, J. A. Bellanca, & Fogarty (Eds.), *If minds matter: A foreword to the future,* Volume II. Palatine, IL: IRI/Skylight Publishing, Inc.

Cox, M. D. (1997) Long-term patterns in a mentoring program for junior faculty: recommendations for practice, *To Improve the Academy,* 16, 225-268.

Deci, E. L., Kasser, T. and Ryan, R. M. (1997) Self-determined teaching: opportunities and obstacles. In J. L. Bess (ed.) *Teaching Well and Liking it.* Baltimore: The Johns Hopkins University Press, 57-70.

Doyle, W. (1983) Academic work. *Review of Educational Research,* 53, 153-199.

Elias, M. J., Zinz, J. E., Weissberg, R. P., Frey, K. S., Greenberg, M. T., Haynes, N. M., Kessler, R., Schwab-Stone, M. E., & Shriver, T. P. (1997). *Promoting social and emotional learning.* Alexandria, VA: Association for the Supervision of Curriculum Development.

Etobicoke Board of Education. (1987). *Making the grade.* Scarborough, ON: Prentice-Hall.

Gardner, H. (1983). *Frames of mind,* New York: Basic Books.

Gelb, M. (1988). *Present yourself.* Torrance, CA: Jaimar Press.

Gilbert, J. P., Keck, K. L., & Simpson, R. D. (1993). Improving the process of education: Total Quality Management for the college classroom. *Innovative Higher Education,* 18 (1), 65-84.

Goleman, D. (1995). *Emotional intelligence.* New York: Bantam Books.

_____. (1998). *Working with Emotional Intelligence.* New York: Bantam Books.

Gronlund, N. E. (1995). *How to write and use instructional objectives.* Englewood Cliffs, NJ: Prentice Hall.

Grunert, J. (1997) *The College Syllabus.* Bolton MA: Anker.

Guskey, T. R. (Ed.). (1996). *ASCD Year Book: Communicating student learning.* Alexandria, VA: Association for Supervision and Curriculum Development.

Harvey, L. & Knight, P. T. (1996) *Transforming higher education.* Buckingham & Philadelphia: Society for Research in Higher Education and Open University Press.

Herman, J. L., Aschbacher, P. R., & Winters, L. (1992). *A practical guide to alternative assessment.* Alexandria, VA: Association for Supervision and Curriculum Development.

Hoffmann, B. (1964). *The tyranny of testing.* New York: Collier Books.

Johnson, C., & Ury, C. (1998). Detecting Internet plagiarism. *The National Teaching and Learning Forum,* 7 (4) 7-8.

Johnson, D. Johnson, R. T., & Holubec, E. J. (1994). *Cooperative learning in the classroom*. Alexandria, VA: Association for Supervision and Curriculum Development.

Jones, E. A. (1996). National and state policies affecting learning expectations. In E. A. Jones (Ed.), *Preparing competent college graduates: Setting new and higher expectations in student learning* (pp. 7-17). San Francisco: Jossey-Bass.

Kagan, S. (1992). *Cooperative learning*. San Juan Capistrano, CA: Resources for Teachers, Inc.

King, M., & Ranallo, J. (1993). *Teaching and assessment strategies for the transition age*. Vancouver: EduServ.

Linn, R. L., & Gronlund, N. E. (1995). *Measurement and assessment in teaching* 7th ed. Upper Saddle River, NJ: Prentice-Hall.

Majesky, D. (1993). Grading should go. *Educational Leadership, 50* (7), 88, 90.

Marton, F., Hounsell, D. and Entwistle, N. (eds.) (1997) *The Experience of learning : implications for teaching and studying in higher education*. Edinburgh: Scottish Academic Press.

Marzano, R. J., Pickering, D., & McTighe, J. (1993). *Assessing student outcomes: Performance assessment using the dimensions of learning model*. Alexandria, VA: Association for Supervision and Curriculum Development.

Morgan, G. (1997). *Images of organization*. (2nd ed.). Thousand Oaks, CA: Sage.

National Council of Teachers of Mathematics. (1989). *Curriculum and evaluation standards for school mathematics*. Reston, VA: Author.

National Teaching and Learning Forum. (1998). Resources. *The National Teaching and Learning Forum, 7* (4), 12. Author.

Nitko, A. J. (1996). *Educational assessment of students*. (2nd ed.). Englewood Cliffs, NJ: Prentice-Hall Inc.

O'Connell Davidson, J. and Layder, J. (1994) *Methods, Sex and Madness*. London: Routledge

O'Neil, C. and Wright, W. A. (1995) *Recording Teaching Accomplishment.* (5th ed.). Halifax NS: Dalhousie University Office of Instructional Development and Technology.

Palomba, C., & Banta, T. (1999). *Assessment essentials*. San Francisco: Jossey-Bass.

Pascarella, E. T. & Terenzini, P. T. (1991). *How college affects students*. San Francisco: Jossey-Bass.

Perkins, D. (1992) *Smart Schools* New York: The Free Press.

Perrone, V. (Ed.). (1991). *Expanding student assessment*. Alexandria, VA: Association for Supervision and Curriculum Development.

Popham, W. J. (1999). *Classroom Assessment: What Teachers Need to Know.* (2nd ed.).Toronto: Allyn and Bacon.

Prosser, M. & Trigwell, K. (1999). *Understanding learning and teaching.* Buckingham & Philadelphia: Society for Research in Higher Education and Open University Press.

Schön, D. A. (1983). *The reflective practitioner.* New York: Basic Books.

Seldin, P., & Associates. (1990). *How administrators can improve teaching.* San Francisco: Jossey-Bass.

_____. (1993). *Successful use of teaching portfolios.* Bolton: Anker Publishing Co.

Smil, V. (1999). *Energies.* Cambridge, MA: Massachusetts Institute of Technology.

Sternberg, R. J, (1997). Successful intelligence. New York: Plume.

Stiggins, R. J. (1997). *Student-centred classroom assessment.* (2nd ed.). Toronto: Maxwell MacMillan.

Weisberg, Knapper, and Wilcox, from the Instructional Development Centre, Queens' University, at Kingston. http://www.queensu.ca/idc/HandBook/semtut.html

Wenger, E. (1998) *Communities of practice: learning, meaning and identity.* Cambridge and New York: Cambridge University Press.

Wiggins, G. P. (1993). *Assessing student performance: Exploring the purpose and limits of testing.* San Francisco: Jossey-Bass.

Willis, S. (1996). ASCD update, 38 (4), 1 & 4.

Wilson, R. J. (1996). *Assessing students in classrooms and schools.* Allyn & Bacon, Scarborough, ON.